D0054127

Living Simply in God's Abundance

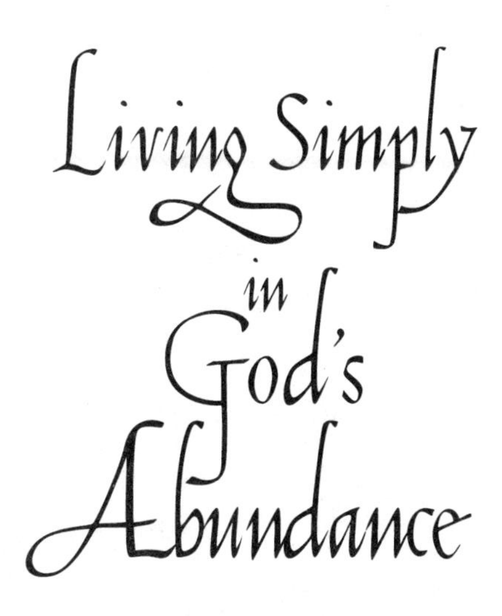

Living Simply in God's Abundance

STRENGTH AND COMFORT FOR THE SEASONS OF A WOMAN'S LIFE

Suzanne Dale Ezell

THOMAS NELSON PUBLISHERS
Nashville
Printed in the United States of America

Published in Nashville, Tennessee, by Thomas Nelson, Inc., Publishers.

Library of Congress Cataloging-in-Publication Data

Ezell, Suzanne.
Living simply in God's abundance : strength and comfort for the seasons of a woman's life / Suzanne Dale Ezell.
p. cm.
ISBN 0-7852-7063-9 (hardcover)
1. Women—Religious life. I. Title.
BV4527.E96 1998
248.8'43—dc21 97-49903
CIP

Printed in the United States of America.

2 3 4 5 6 BVG 03 02 01 00 99 98

To the generations of women
who make me who I am:
my mother, Mary Dale,
and my grandmothers,
Allie Dyer and Fannie Dale,
who are my past and my roots;
my two beautiful daughters,
Sara and Melanie,
who are my present;
and to my unborn granddaughters,
who will be my future and my wings.

Contents

Acknowledgments

This book grew from a seed planted by book planner extraordinaire, Dave Shepherd. Dave and I each grew up in parsonages in the West Texas area, then crossed paths years later in Nashville. He and I worked together on another book, and he remembered the up and down trials our family had traversed. He thought perhaps the telling of those stories would fit a niche and suggested the idea to me. Dave is a clever and experienced book planner and book seller, and he and his wife, Betty, have been profound family friends for many years. Thank you, Dave, for believing in the story.

Next Thomas Nelson's expert, visionary editor, Janet Thoma, designed, refined, and articulated the book idea into a doable project. Todd Ross, Janet's managing editor, was my hand holder, offering comfort and encouragement as the writing moved along. My thanks to both of these very professional and proficient people.

With the deepest love and appreciation, I thank my husband, my children, my mother, my friends, and my larger extended family. As I have searched to discover what matters most in life, all I can find are reflections of these people who matter.

The Seasons of a Woman's Life

As my pen moves across these pages, I sit in a quiet place in the Autumn of my life. It is like sitting on a comfortable, grassy knoll where I can see both behind me and in front of me—a 360-degree view. I can look back to the Spring of my life, when I was so naive, so wanting to please, so unaware of the road before me. I can look back to the Summer of my life, when I made a family and began to chart my own course. I can also visualize the coming Winter of my life, with its health challenges, its loss of power and independence. I'll need to prepare carefully for that.

A woman's life divides nicely into four seasons. Major life passages break up the years into segments of time, with each season having specific tasks to be accomplished, goals to be met, and wisdom to be gleaned. As you live and grow and pass from one season to another, it can be a time of reflection and soul-searching for the coming season.

Spring

I see the Spring of a woman's life as her childhood and youth. It is from this season that you first look out at the wonder of the universe. From the warmth, support, and security of your family of origin, you begin to make sense of the world in which you will spend your life. It is here that you glimpse the complexity of life, then venture forth to experiment and explore.

The tasks of Spring can be imposing: this is where you nurture your roots and acquire your values. Your family of origin makes the rules you live by, and by the late Spring you must decide if these rules will indeed be your own life's rules or if they need to be abandoned or modified for a more workable set.

Spring provides the climate, the nourishment, and the soil from which your womanhood will blossom. The passage during late Spring can be a dramatic and tumultuous event. This journey requires a letting go, a breaking away, a leaving of the familiar. A young woman in late Spring needs to claim a measure of autonomy all her own. A sad passage is one where a young woman simply transfers her source of authority from her parents to her new husband and never claims independence for herself. This sets up a situation where the Spring season is never closed out and Summer simply has to fit in around unresolved needs.

Summer

As a young woman stands alone and begins a life on her own terms, in her own dwelling, she passes into the Summer of her life. This may come with a first career, a marriage, or other independent living plan. For this to be a true Summer season, it needs to have a purpose and a plan with clear goals and objectives. (A young woman with one of Dad's credit cards still in her pocket is continuing to enjoy Spring.)

Summer is trial and error, joy and sorrow, some gentleness and some toughness, some confidence and some uncertainty, some peace and some turmoil, cherishing those things that embellish life, and rejecting those things that diminish it—then taking all the pieces, putting them together, and making a life. This is a season of unlimited potential.

These are the years of childbearing, family building, and/or career launching. Summer often requires a measure of self-denial for women—giving to children, giving to the marriage, giving to the company, giving to extended family.

The pitfalls of Summer are these: getting lost in the shuffle and forgetting to be good to yourself first. Summer tasks have a tendency to overpower and grind you to fatigue if you're not careful.

The tasks of Summer include finding your inner self, an inner quietness, a kind of wisdom of the heart. This is the place you meet God, the place your flashes of intuition and invention come from.

Summer is making your signature in the world, creating the image of who you are in the universe. It is the time to find your own special identity, something beyond the roles you are known by, something in yourself you can recognize and respect and live with in some degree of comfort. Summer draws to a close as the family you made begins its transition, and you begin to feel the shift. As the children grow up, leave home, and establish their own domains, your life advances into the Autumn of your years.

Autumn

For women who have enjoyed Summer, the passage into Autumn has the promise of the very best years of your life. Women who have failed to negotiate the warm, free-flowing waters of Summer will enter the Autumn years feeling unprotected and ill prepared for the transition. I think these are the women who cannot face their children having lives of their own, who cry that they are "no longer needed," and who refuse to go forward with grace and dignity.

Autumn is the true harvesttime of life. All the positive growth you experienced in Summer, the relationships you invested in, the diligent child raising you tended to, the hours and effort you invested in a career, now return to you as a reward. You can sit back and rejoice in the bounty, the successes, the goodness of life.

There *is* life after the empty nest—lots of good life. And now you also have the life experiences, the intelligence, and the desire to try new things, to learn something new just for the sheer joy of it. Many women feel a beautiful sense of adventure and are ready to try new careers, or go back to school, or forge new relationships.

This season offers the most fertile years of spiritual growth. The personal maturity level of Autumn puts you in touch with more meaningful ways to relate to God.

Autumn has some specific tasks. You must begin your personal essay on death and dying. This is *not* a morbid fixation on the end of life, but an attempt to shake hands with death, to make friends with the foe. Death is a part of living. It needs to be looked at, walked up to, and embraced as a part of God's plan. The Autumn of your life will begin to include deaths of friends and aging family members. Learn to make these events celebrations of life.

Another task of Autumn is to make peace with the aging process. Aging is a fact—short-term memory disruption, wrinkles, changing body shape, a little slowing of pace. Bend in to the changes. It's OK! There is a comfort, a warmth, a deep richness in the aging process that makes you infinitely more interesting, more fascinating, and more fulfilled than ever before in your life.

The old saying that "youth is a gift, but age is a work of art" is so true! There is nothing more elegant and appealing than an Autumn woman acting and looking her age. Mature beauty exudes personal power and poise. Celebrate the harvest!

Winter

It is difficult to say exactly when the passage from Autumn to Winter occurs. It may be the same question as, When are you old?

One fact is absolute: chronological age has less to do with this passage than any other. I believe the onset of Winter coincides with a life illness that begins to take its toll on your mind or body, an illness that changes your day-to-day life.

Winter is a gift of time. Even in declining health you can continue to enjoy life. Your immune system can be tricked into believing that life is not over, that you still have important things to do. Positive attitudes, exercise, staying active, and growing spiritually can all work together to extend the Winter years significantly. Set the standard for living every day to the fullest, and you may discover that Winter is the sweetest season of all.

Enjoy Your Seasons

My goal in writing this book has been to help you recognize and enjoy each season of your life and to challenge you to keep stretching and growing no matter where you are on life's journey. Perhaps some little nugget of truth I've learned along the way will be a blessing to you in your walk with God.

These eighty-six devotionals have been culled from my life experiences and my observations about biblical women. In the following pages you will encounter word pictures of each of the four seasons of life. They are placed in random order, so you will keep coming across something applicable to your situation, whether you are still basking in the late Spring or Summer of life, celebrating the rich harvesttime of Autumn, or fast approaching the maturity of Winter.

I pray these words will bring you strength and comfort as you face the challenges of life. May you know God's abundance and the blessing of living simply in the light of His goodness and grace.

THE WALK BEGINS

Instead of looking at life as a narrowing funnel, see it ever widening to choose the things we want to do, to take the wisdom we've learned and create something. —LIZ CARPENTER

In 1957 thirty-seven of us graduated from a small high school in West Texas. To give you an idea of the remoteness of our town, it was the only town in the county, deep in the sheep-ranching area of the state. Occasionally we went to the closest small town, forty-two miles away, to attend basketball games. Once every three to four weeks we drove eighty-five miles to San Angelo to buy groceries.

Girls married as soon as graduation was over and moved out to the ranches to have babies and cook for the ranch hands. I escaped this dismal destiny because I was an outsider to the culture. My father was not a rancher; he was the preacher at the church on Main Street. So the rules for me were different.

We didn't have television most of my high school years. The local newspaper was published weekly and consisted mostly of ranch news. But the radio and *Life* magazine gave us ideas about what the outside world had to offer. I read where some women did things besides keep house and have babies. I also heard there was a group of women who thought the female population might not be getting a fair deal in society. They talked about wages and opportunities for women. But the terms they used were harsh, the rhetoric was tough, and the leaders looked like women trying to be men. The life they championed was a world away from the life of a West Texas woman.

Make no mistake about it, however. West Texas women could work sheep with the best of the men. They could hunt, handle a gun, field-dress a deer, and communicate with ranch hands as well as anyone. But a woman's place was very clearly defined, and in the last analysis she had few, if any, rights of decision.

I tell this story not because it is a vastly interesting story (although my kids are usually enamored with the part about no TV), but because it is a classic cameo of where and how many of us start the Walk.

In those growing-up years in the parsonage, the rules of conduct—right and wrong—were clearly set and clearly communicated. There were no gray areas. "Don't drink, don't dance, don't smoke. Always obey your parents!" These were my parents' rules, and I assumed they were God's rules as well.

My dad was a pastor type in every sense of the word. He was large and dignified and always stood on the "right" side of any question. He set the rules for our family and Mother was the enforcer. The perils of God's wrath were vividly described to me at an early age. And the possibility of sure and irrevocable punishment remained a constant deterrent to many a desire. I was well into my college years before I realized that Deity and my dad were not one and the same.

Negative? No. Harsh? No, not really. Narrow? Yes. But a great place to start the Walk! A rock-solid foundation. The basics of a strong belief system were firmly set in place. A Bible-based belief system—we could quote a Scripture verse for every letter of the alphabet, and I could name all sixty-six books of the Bible in sequence.

Yes, I had the tools to work with. And with those tools, I set out on a long and sometimes difficult walk.

The Summer of My Life

Goals are a joint effort process: getting in touch with our heart and setting a course; then depending on and being willing for God to direct us one step at a time. —SHEILA WEST

At age twenty-four I traded my family of origin for a family I would create myself. It happened while I was an assistant student director of a denominational ministry on the campus of the University of Texas at Austin.

I look back now and marvel at my naïveté, especially compared to young people today. My beginning had been humble and underexposed. When I reflect on that big campus teeming with curious philosophies, I wonder how I kept my head on straight enough to survive.

Our student ministry worked closely with the local church, which was programmed to reach the college population. No wonder the campus ministry person and the church youth minister found each other and then married two years later.

Since all I had ever known was living in a church-related family, marrying a church staff person was familiar territory. But the surprise was on me. Three months after we married, Mancil was called to work at the national denominational publishing house in Nashville. The Lord knew what He was doing, but it took me a long time to see. It may have been one of *Mancil's* lifelong dreams to move to Nashville, but for me it meant leaving my family, my home, and my native state. I followed that moving van for more than a thousand miles with tears streaming down both cheeks.

Moving to Nashville was a staggering culture shock. I agreed to stay just for a few years—three at the most—until Mancil could get this foolishness out of his system and we could get back to Texas where we belonged.

When we bought a little house, I had all the new carpet bound into room-size rugs instead of installed wall to wall—so I could take them back to Texas when we moved home. My family laughs now and declares that I kept the luggage by the back door so I could get to it at a moment's notice. Mancil tells that at my insistence we backed the car into the garage so I could make a faster getaway back to Texas whenever he gave the word.

It isn't that I disliked Tennessee. Actually I loved it. God had chosen a beautiful and flourishing place for us to live. Opportunities for teaching and writing were abundant. It was just so far from my family. And there were all those trees! Big trees, with long hanging limbs and branches that blocked the sky. I could never see the horizon. I thought I would suffocate to death with all the foliage.

I can remember so vividly the very afternoon I realized I was in Tennessee to stay. By that time our three babies had been born. The first baby, Chase, had been born in Texas. I went home several weeks before the delivery so I could give birth to a Texan.

Sitting in my big wicker rocker that day, I counted the years. We had been in Nashville for seven years. We had a fun old house we were restoring. Mancil loved working at the publishing house. I had a job I enjoyed. Then it hit me: I was not going to move back to Texas—I was in Nashville for good! How could this be?

"Dear God, did You forget about me here?" I asked.

It had just never come to my awareness that God had any plan for me whatsoever outside of Texas. There is no such thing as a former Texan, you know.

But now, thirty-five years after I crossed the Mississippi River for the first time in my life, I can say that I am a Texan who lives in Tennessee and loves it. The trees that nearly suffocated me are now beautiful and nurturing to me. Growing things in Tennessee is so easy. You just stick a little green sprout of something into the ground, and God turns it into an exquisite flower.

And on that day, all those years ago, sitting in my antique rocker, I began the Summer of my life. Living in this lush, green land, we made a new family. Tennessee was a good place to put down my own roots.

FAITH AND POWER:
GIFTS FOR THE WALK

'Twant me, 'twas the Lord. I always told him, "I trust you. I don't know where to go or what to do, but I expect you to lead me," and he always did. —HARRIET TUBMAN

Talk to any Christian who has been through a valley, a deep life trauma, and you will hear much the same thing: "I don't know how I did it, but somehow I made it through."

The resilience of the human spirit is amazing indeed. The recuperative response within each of us is so incredible that at times we surprise even ourselves.

There is no question that life is difficult and uncertain. In the blink of an eye, life can come crashing down around us like a rain of brimstone. Whether these crises come at a bedside, a graveside, a roadside, or in a marriage, a relationship, an office, or a church setting, the results can leave us devastated—weak-kneed and shattered.

These are the moments faith is made of. The Bible supports this, and I have seen it time after time in my own life and in others'. The more we need faith, the more faith we are given. The more we completely trust God, the deeper that trust grows.

Faith and power are gifts that go hand in hand, and they come from the source of all power, the Holy Spirit. Call it what you will—stamina, courage, tenacity, hanging on, resilience—it is that touch of divine miracle when we feel like we can't take another step. But then we do. We were somehow strengthened beyond our understanding to stand a little longer, to take one more move forward, or to go a little beyond the totally helpless feeling of being out of control.

God's gifts of faith and power are always adequate, no matter how desperate our situation has become. Exhaustion, frustration, and tragedy may have us burdened down so that we despair of ever being free again. The pain may be unrelenting, the loss overwhelming, the loneliness damning. But God's power is great enough for our deepest desperation.

You *can* go on. You *can* pick up the pieces and start anew. You *can* face your fears. You *can* find peace in the rubble. You *can* have courage. There *is* healing for your soul.

My pastor gave an illustration that is the perfect picture of faith: You arrive at the airport, baggage in both hands. You approach the closed door and wonder how you can get the door open with your arms so full of baggage. How, indeed? All that is necessary is to take one more step. The doors open automatically.

Or suppose you are walking on a very dark night using only a small flashlight. The light makes a circle immediately in front of you. Only as you take a step does the light move out in front.

Do you see? Take just one more step and you will be given the faith and the power to add another step, and another. You grow as you go.

TWICE BLESSED

Being a mother is rewarding to one's female instincts, trying to one's nerves, physically exhausting, emotionally both frustrating and satisfying, and above all, not to be undertaken lightly. —DR. MARGARET RAPHAEL

The days and years of early marriage flew by. My babies were only young for such a short time. Twice it was my joy to hold in my arms and look with awe into the face of a newborn son. How God could create these tiny persons and send them to us to love and cherish seemed to be the astonishment of my life. There was always magic and mystery in that tiny baby bundle—those little fingers gripping mine, that beautiful little bow of a mouth always ready to eat. And they are a part of me—maybe the best of me—that will remain after my life is over on earth. My hope of immortality.

Two little boys: my firstborn son, Chase, then two and a half years later, Jason. Both were solid, stocky boys with blond hair and twinkling eyes, the kind that made you wonder what they had been up to. I cherished each day with those baby boys. I knew that as we said good night at the end of each twenty-four hours, that day was gone forever. Each little munchkin would certainly grow into more stages that would have its own delights, but no two days would offer the same adventures.

Chase had Fred, a well-worn blue teddy bear that was as much a part of him as his two arms, until the day he shared it with a new puppy—and poor Fred went to his final resting place. You might say Fred was all to pieces there at the end.

Jason had a red-felt "cow-buddy" hat that he wore everywhere—sometimes with clothes, sometimes without. No matter. From his earliest steps he learned to waddle down to the creek with a stick and a string to "go fishing." It took a few years for him to catch on that he also needed a hook and some bait to make the process work. But for a few years, he was happy and content with the empty string.

Each night, Mancil and I would stand and look at those little sleeping boys. They played until they were so tired they almost fell asleep in midair. We were filled with emotion for the divineness of it all—the miracle of their minds, grasping and learning so much every day, their beauty, their excitement about life, their buoyancy. I wept for the joy of them.

Even today, when one them comes home for a visit, I look at that six-foot-tall, good-looking young man raiding the refrigerator or stretched out on the sofa, and I still thank God for the miracle of it all.

Special Delivery

If God is here for us and not elsewhere, then in fact this place is holy and this moment is sacred.

—ISABEL ANDERS

For the third time, I woke up in a hospital recovery room, semiaware of the busyness around me. Back in those olden days, twenty-five years ago, we mercifully had not heard of natural childbirth. We were offered all the nice painkilling drugs we wanted, so I had opted for sedation.

Two nurses were talking. "I dread when this one wakes up," one of them said. "Her baby didn't make it."

I carefully peeped out of one eye to see if they were talking about me. No, thank goodness. But I instantly felt a profound sorrow for the mother who yet had to hear this news.

About that time my dear husband walked into the room. "We have a girl!" he announced. "She is beautiful. They said there is a little problem with her arms and legs. But I'm sure everything is going to be all right." Always the eternal optimist, Mancil.

Trouble? What kind of trouble? I wondered. In my fog, I couldn't begin to grasp what that might mean.

I don't remember how much time elapsed, but finally the pediatrician came in. "We have a little problem," he said. "We're not quite sure what. I haven't seen this exact situation before. There is a specialist coming in." The doctor's eyes began to well up with tears, and he hurriedly left the room.

The doctor was our good friend. He had held my hand through the usual mishaps of two little boys: stitches, dehydration, ear infections, and all sorts of things.

Something wrong with our baby girl?! A blessed numbness settled over us. *No way! Not my baby,* I thought *They will just have to fix it. They can do wonders these days.*

We waited. Half a day went by. We made a few calls to the grandparents, never mentioning the prospects of the unspecified trouble. By supper time Mancil had to go home to our two little boys, who were waiting with the neighbors. I was left alone to sort through the medical information.

I wanted to see my baby girl. But the nurse kindly explained that would not be possible—she was in an incubator. She explained in a very patronizing way that the doctor would be in soon. "Just be patient," she chirped.

Hours later, an eternity later, the specialist came in. He pulled up a chair and sat down. I could tell we had a lot to talk about.

"Your daughter has osteogenesis imperfecta," he said gently. "Sometimes it is called brittle bone disease. Both of her legs were broken and grew back before she was born. She has one broken leg and one broken arm now. We are hesitant to take her out of the incubator to handle her because we could break more bones. We don't know much about the disease. There isn't anything we can do. There is no treatment. She probably won't walk; she may not even be able to sit alone. All we know is that with good home care, she can learn to do some things. The only ray of hope is that all of the children who have this disease are very bright, very outgoing, and very happy children, in spite of the way they have to live. She will have a lot of broken bones, and each fracture will be painful and crippling."

A long silence followed. Wisely, he sat quietly and let this all soak in. As I pondered the future of pain and suffering, I spoke in a whisper. "I have one question to start with, but you must promise not to call the psychiatrist if I ask you."

"OK. Sure."

"Can she die now?" I whispered.

"No," he said, just as quietly.

"Then I must set about making a plan. Can you help me?"

"Not really. It will mostly be up to you and your husband. I will help you find a good orthopedist. One of the country's leading authorities on this disease lives right here in Nashville."

The doctor left and I was alone. I called Mancil at home and tried to relay the grim information. We both wished we could be together at this moment. But parenting called us in two different locations.

It is hard to write about what happened next, simply because I don't have words to explain. To this day, I'm not sure I know what happened.

The room became filled with a mix of panic, fear, devastation, disbelief, cold terror, grief, pain, despair, and loneliness. That is a lot to contend with. All these feelings and thoughts racked my mind and pounded my body. I cried, I mourned, I prayed for it all to go away. A raging storm thundered in the very depths of my soul.

After a while, I paused to rest between the crashing waves of sorrow, and something happened. In the midst of the storm came a voice so calm, so clear, and so audible that I sat up quickly to see who was in the room with me. I could see no one.

The voice seemed to come from the corner of the room. I felt a presence I cannot begin to describe. A calming spirit filled the room and took hold of the storm. The Voice called my name.

"Suzanne, the baby you have just been given is a divine gift, like all My babies. With this special baby I will be able to show you more about My love than you could know in any other way. Do not be afraid, for I will walk beside you every step of the way. I have given you the tools you will need to do the job. Lean on Me."

The Voice left. I never heard it again in exactly that same way. In its place was a comfort and calmness I had not known. I lay very still and tried to take in all that had happened so far. A tiny baby facing an uncertain future. An audible promise of divine grace and mercy. I knew I was on holy ground.

"Dear Lord, I'll try. With your help, I'll try."

TOOLS FOR THE JOURNEY

Each story is like a new challenge or a new adventure, and I don't find help anywhere, or look for it anywhere except inside. —EUDORA WELTY

Mancil and I both felt the same. We had been chosen, handpicked to parent three wonderful children. Each child was unique and brought a package of special pleasures to the family.

But we knew that tiny Baby Sara would bring a dimension to the group that would change our lives forever. In addition to the joys and benefits of having a little sister, there would be a responsibility given to us as parents and to two big brothers. The opportunities would call for strength, wisdom, and coping on all our parts. Watching a tiny child suffer would deplete our reserves time and time again.

The Voice in the hospital room had left me with an assurance that we had been given the resources we would need, so we began to focus on these strengths and determine what we had to work with.

First and foremost, we had a legion of nurturing family and friends. The outpouring of care and concern was overwhelming. Cards, letters, visits, and phone calls from all over the United States assured us of love and prayers. What a world of blessing. Our family and friends believed in us!

Second, we had each other. This was not a task I would want to tackle alone. God had given me a caring and supportive co-parent who was not afraid of challenges. Together we were, and are, strong.

Mancil is highly gifted at always looking on the bright side of any situation. Somewhere he can find a glimmer of good. There were situations to come when that glimmer became more and more difficult to find, but he always managed to keep us focused on hope.

Third, we were both very resourceful and creative. My grandmother had a saying, "You can't make a silk purse out of a sow's ear." But *we* could have, and it would have been the best, most beautiful silk purse ever. Our ability to create was a gift we used to good advantage. It became a mainstay in the years to come.

Like the year Sara was in the hospital in a large traction frame over the Fourth of July holiday. We used red, white, and blue crepe paper to decorate the whole bed like a parade float. We got hamburgers, sneaked the boys into her room, and had the best Fourth of July picnic any family could have. People came from all over the hospital to see.

Next, we had been given a sustaining corporate environment, with adequate medical insurance. We would have financial support for doctors, hospitals, and assistive devices. What a blessing!

Finally, we all had each other. I cannot say enough about the value and importance of a family unit. The absolute glorious gift of two beautiful brothers to help love and care for our Baby Sara has been grace in its purest and most divine form. How could we ever wish for more? A family of five is a wonderful system of support for every need, pain, or fear that could come our way.

Another unbelievable resource came in the form of the medical doctors in Nashville. We were so fortunate to live near a major medical center where there were renowned specialists in Sara's disease. We did not have to search the world over for medical help.

And most important, our resource gifts included a sense of divine purpose. We absolutely could have no other idea than to think that our family could be sustained by God's own plan. He had taken a set of circumstances that occurred, given us specific tools to work with, and together we walked to new depths of love and trust.

WHAT IS OLD?

Growing old is something we all think about. For some of us, those thoughts come more frequently. It's easy to think you're eternally young if you're slim and trim, with a head full of hair. But when those laugh lines around your eyes turn into crevasses and the hair on your head turns silver, . . . then we're forced to face the reality that we're not teenagers anymore. —BERNIE SHEAHAN

How do you know what year you turn *old?* Is it the year Mama spends most of the time looking for her glasses and usually finds them on the top of her head? Is it the year Dad not only loses the car keys but can't remember where he left the car?

Or does *old* look like eighty-five-year-old Aunt Margaret on her way to France for the fifth time?

You can join the senior citizens' center when you're fifty-five. And you can start getting discounts at the cafeteria when you're fifty-five. But you can't get Social Security until you're sixty-two or sixty-five. So how do you know for sure when you're old?

General Douglas MacArthur said, "Nobody grows old by merely living a number of years. People grow old only by deserting their ideas. . . . You are as young as your self-confidence, as old as your despair."

After observing many, many seniors in various processes of aging, I think there are three very defined clues that point to a person's being old.

Old is when you lose your dream. That could be at age eighty, or age fifty, or age thirty-nine, or any age at all. Hopes and dreams for a bright future are what keep people young and vibrant. My good friend Rick reroofed his house when he was ninety-seven—*by himself.* And wondered about the guarantee on the materials he used. My grandfather and grandmother remodeled their home when they were eighty-five and shopped to get a carpet with a long-wear finish.

Old is when you start turning in on yourself. When your world shrinks inward. When your own stories or daily health report takes up most of your conversation. Young people—at any age—are focused outward, on what's going on around town, on the news, what's happening tomorrow, and next door, and in Japan. When you're old, you let your world shrink until it is only the size of you.

Old is when you look backward more than you look forward. The "good old days" are gone—if they ever existed at all. The "way things used to be" is not the way things are now. Thank goodness. My sweet little mother-in-law used to cook three meals a day on a wood-burning stove. The only air conditioning in their home was the breeze that blew through the cracks between the floorboards. I am glad *those* good old days are gone forever. I would not have survived. Look at how good things are now. What a great time to be alive! Look forward to the best that is yet to be.

Stay alive! On a moment-to-moment, day-to-day basis embrace life, accept challenges, learn something new, change, and grow. Come to terms with the person you are now—whether pleasant or unpleasant, active or reflective—no matter the number of years you have lived.

> *This day I call heaven and earth as witnesses against you that I have set before you life and death, blessings and curses. Now choose life, so that you and your children may live and that you may love the LORD your God, listen to his voice, and hold fast to him. For the LORD is your life, and he will give you many years in the land he swore to give to your fathers, Abraham, Isaac and Jacob.* Deuteronomy 30:19–20 NIV

DOES IT STILL HURT?

As painful as memories can be, they can also be the stepping stones for personal growth.

—BERNIE SHEAHAN

Look back. Look way back. Search through your memory bank for the cobwebs—the unhappy times, the painful memories of the past, the ghosts that still come out at odd times to haunt you.

Does a certain memory still bring you pain? Do you still shudder with a chill down your spine when you think about it? If so, this is likely an unresolved situation and one that continues to pour poison into your system. It is a memory that is still influencing your judgment.

Let's try to fix it.

Select a quiet place to think. Bring up the very sad memory in your mind. Think through every detail, just as you have done dozens of times before. How did it feel? Who was there? What was said? Were there smells associated with the event? What was the weather like?

I was six years old when my father decided to go to seminary. He left his job and temporarily got a room in Ft. Worth to attend classes. Mother moved with us three children to my grandmother's house in West Texas. In those very olden days, adults didn't take much time to explain goings-on to children. I realized that something very drastic was happening to our family, but I had no idea what.

I was at school in the cafeteria when Daddy came to tell me good-bye. It was raining, and I still remember those cafeteria smells. I thought he was leaving forever—maybe because he didn't love me or maybe because I had been bad, I wasn't sure which. Naturally, I didn't share these feelings with anyone. I didn't want anyone else to know my terrible secret—that I had caused my father to leave home.

Of course, the real truth was that he was going away briefly to attend seminary to prepare for a ministry. We would see him often, and we were all reunited as soon as he was through with his school work. But I didn't know all of that on the front end. And the fact that it turned out all right never quite measured up to the trauma of that good-bye day in the cafeteria.

It was years before I could eat in a cafeteria without getting deathly sick, and rainy days overwhelmed me mercilessly.

As I played and replayed this memory, it always made me sad beyond tears. The feelings associated with this memory followed me into marriage. Every time Mancil left on a business trip, I was devastated. I felt I was being abandoned. Since he traveled a lot, I had a difficult time.

But here is the help. As you have replayed your moment, detail by detail, now step back and stop the record at midpoint. Take the scene up to a certain point, then stop the action.

Use your imagination and rewrite a new ending to the script. Make the story turn out to your advantage. Create a new memory. Tape over the first ending and replace it with a happy ending.

Now, each time you accidentally pull up this memory, carefully plug in the good ending for yourself. Healing old memories takes time and determination. Reprogramming is step one in the process.

STRESS BUSTER

There is not a woman on earth who does not face a challenge with stress. Our roles are so demanding. The hours are long and sometimes rewards are few.

One of my partners in an antique booth once told me I had an uncanny knack for making anything and everything stressful. I invariably set deadlines that are too short, set goals that are too high, and expect absolute perfection from myself and everyone around me. You talk about stress! Those are three surefire stress builders.

Throughout this book are short Stress Busters—suggestions for five-minute chill-outs. Usually it will be something you can do anywhere, anytime. Use these busters to defuse a stress attack in midair or use them on the front end, the moment you feel the back of your neck starting to tighten.

Whisper a Chant. Close your eyes and whisper one of the following phrases. Repeat the phrase slower each time, taking a deep breath between each repeat.

"Peggy Piper picked pink pedal pushers."

"Find peace among the papers."

Focus on the movement of your lips and mouth as you whisper the words. Feel the rhythm of your breathing. After repeating the phrase several times, sit quietly for a few minutes and let an imaginary, lightweight cloak of peace fall gently around your shoulders.

THE WEDDING GUEST

There is nothing so secular that it cannot be sacred, and that is one of the deepest messages of the Incarnation. —MADELEINE L'ENGLE

Picture a little Eastern town, not too far off the coast of the beautiful Mediterranean Sea. The town is placed strategically on a caravan route between the sea and the imperial city of Tiberias. So the drama and excitement of frequent camel caravans coming through the town kept Cana lively and full of adventure.

The houses were nestled close together on a slope. Pomegranate groves, gnarled olive trees, and brilliantly colored wildflowers gave the little town the look of a tourist brochure.

Family life was simple in Cana, gently folding one generation into the next, year after year. Nothing changing. Life governed mostly by tradition.

Events such as weddings were celebrated with abandon in Cana. Weddings were big social events for the entire town—everyone was included. The groom was the host and bore all the expenses. Needless to say, throwing a feast for the entire town could be costly. As expected, women relatives of the groom's family gathered from far and near to help prepare the food. They worked for days making the delicacies to be consumed by reveling guests.

On one special occasion, described in the second chapter of the Gospel of John, Mary was a part of this working-relative group. She went to Cana a few days before the wedding to assist in the wedding preparations. Mary was a widow by this time, and according to the life expectancy standards of that day, she may have been one of the older women of the family.

Jesus, who by tradition had become the head of the household for Mary, had been gone from home for many weeks. Jesus had spent the time being baptized and preparing Himself for His ministry. Mary perhaps had been getting snippets of this news from friends but, no doubt, longed for more information. Then word came that Jesus was planning to attend the Cana wedding.

Mary was anxious to see her son. Had He been eating well? Did He have a place to stay? How was the ministry going? I like to speculate just how much Mary knew and understood by this point. Did Jesus discuss things with His mom? Did He talk to her about His plans, His calling, His direction?

The tradition of the times might indicate a "no" to these questions. Women were seldom included in important conversations. But I like to think that Mary and her son had a special understanding about His reason for being on earth. After all, Mary had been the very first person to be in on the plan. So as a special player in this drama, a part of her would be open and accepting of the mission. But mothers everywhere would know that a part of Mary was very anxious and concerned for the safety of her son.

I wish we had more information about this wedding meeting and their conversation, but all we have recorded is a simple exchange with a profound outcome.

The wedding ceremony had taken place at the synagogue earlier and now the wedding guests had all gathered at the groom's home for the party. The music was lively, the guests were feasting, the wine was flowing, and the wedding party was merry. It was a magnificent occasion.

But then, a small glitch. The host ran out of refreshments. How embarrassing! The whispers spread through the crowd: "No more wine." A blight on the groom! He couldn't provide a decent wedding for his bride. A cultural *faux pas*.

Mary went to Jesus. "They have no wine," she said. Just a simple statement. Mary didn't bother to explain what she expected from Jesus. She didn't organize the solution. She didn't tell Him what to do. She just stated a fact with the belief He would do what was necessary.

The next exchange is a most curious glimpse into the mother/son connection. "Woman, what does your concern have to do with Me? My hour is not yet come." Jesus had a higher calling and a larger mission than to make a bigger party for a bride and groom.

We're not given much insight into the ambiance of the moment, but apparently Mary was not fazed by the harsh remark. She never hesitated; moving right along she said to the servants, "Whatever He says to you, do it."

And Jesus turned the contents of the water pots into wine so that the big party could continue. He did just what Mary wanted Him to do.

My question is, How did Mary do that? How did she get Jesus to reschedule His divine debut and perform a miracle for a wedding feast?

Was it her tone of voice? Was it a unique mother look, a hard stare that showed one eyebrow raised? Was it her unwavering faith in the Son of God? Mary had taken an obscure community occurrence and with her request and determination turned it into a divine, historical event that would be told and retold for thousands of years to come. Jesus yielded to His mother's plea and took an irreversible step into eternity.

What should we make of this significant encounter between mother and son? Whatever the unspoken message was between them, they ended the evening on good terms. Because after the wedding they all left together and went to Capernaum—Jesus, Mary, His brothers, and the disciples.

Perhaps where Mary and Jesus intersected, we see Him being fully human and fully divine. His humanity left Him vulnerable to His mother's requests, needs, and pleas. He seemed to feel protective and caring toward Mary. But His divine purpose called Him to look at a bigger picture. Perhaps Mary still had a lot to learn too. We don't have records of her making any further requests. Maybe they talked and renegotiated rules for their adult relationship.

That's a position recognized by any mother of an adult son—renegotiating relationships. Gone is the dependence. Gone is the need to please. Gone is the need for direction. In the place of this are two adults, with an intense history, meeting on new territory.

Letting go of sons is very different from letting go of daughters. There came that moment with each of my sons when I was virtually looking into the face of a stranger—that grown-up son. He resembles a child I once had. He even bears some family resemblance. But he is a man, independent of me and needing almost nothing from me.

A woman can teach her son the basics of life, but she cannot teach her son to be a man. A mother has to let go of a son and proudly watch as he walks away from her—never to return in exactly the same way again. Unless a mother can truly and sincerely complete this letting-go experience, she risks the emotional crippling of her son.

I'd like to talk to Mary to see what it was like being the mother to the Savior, knowing there would be so much suffering and persecution. To me, she set the standard for mothers down through the ages by doing her job and then letting go.

It's Just a Waste of Time

Leave old or new ideas where they prove harmful. Leave the bad for the good. Leave good things for better things. But leave when it is appropriate or required for the development of noble character. Then leave well. Leave deliberately. — BARBARA ROBERTS PINE

Jason got in the car after kindergarten on Monday afternoon during the third week of school. He handed me all of the lunch money I had given him that morning.

"I won't be needing this," he announced.

"You didn't want to buy a lunch ticket for this week? You want to start taking your lunch in your new lunchbox?" I probed very carefully.

"Nope! I won't be eating at school any more," he said as emphatically as a five year old could.

I sat silent for a minute and prayed for wisdom. I could tell we were headed into stormy waters.

"Not eating at school, huh? What's up?" I tried to sound a little on the nonchalant side.

"It's very simple," he explained. "I won't need a lunch ticket or a lunchbox because I am not going back!"

His little voice was calm and even, but very firm.

I decided to use my best active listening skills so I could get as much of the story as possible before I pronounced any judgment on the plan. I said, "Hmm. Never going back, huh?"

"Right on!" he said. "Not *ever* going back to that school and *never* going back to that teacher! She taught us our name and address on the first day of school. She has taught us the same thing every day since. I learned all she had to teach on the first day. So I don't need to go back!"

Then he turned sideways in the front seat of the car, narrowed his eyes to slits, lowered his voice for emphasis, pointed a little fat finger at me and said, "I tell you, Mom, if you were there, you wouldn't like it either."

Silence. Words just failed me. I had met the teacher, and frankly I had to agree with Jason. She didn't seem too happy about being a teacher, and I could easily believe that her classroom would not be a happy experience.

So what to do? My son—a kindergarten dropout! What would people say?

My precious little blond-haired, middle child. So together. So sure of himself. Always walking to the beat of his own distant drummer. How I love him for that! It takes a lot of courage to live life on your own terms.

Jason and I did strike a deal that kindergarten year. We enrolled him two days a week in a private kindergarten. Then he stayed home with Baby Sara and me for three days each week. We all loved every minute of that satisfying year.

Parents don't always have all the answers, even though we like to act as if we do. Sometimes God gives us exceptional little children who seem to be endowed with a unique wisdom and a real understanding about what's right and what isn't. To miss these profound morsels by overparenting is a shame.

I learned a lot from Jason that year and in the years to come. Then, and to this day, he lives by four very simple rules:

1. Always play fair.
2. Stand firm for what you truly believe.
3. Stand up for people who need help.
4. Never waste time or energy investing in a useless project.

THE FIVE-AND-TEN-CENT STORE

Memories are crucial to our existence. Without them, we wouldn't know who we are. Memories give us our own personal history, a history that defines us and gives substance to our being.

—BERNIE SHEAHAN

During the ancient days of my childhood, living without TV was not the only hardship we endured. There were no shopping malls, no Kmarts, Wal-Marts, or Home Depots. And no stores were open on Sunday—none! Sunday was a day of rest; even bicycle riding was suspect. So was playing baseball, or going to movies, or playing cards. Can you imagine? Fun that *was* allowed included visiting with friends, neighbors, and family; driving around town; making homemade ice cream; and playing in the yard.

Saturdays were our days of riotous fun—like walking downtown to the five-and-ten-cent store. In our little West Texas town we had a small, locally owned grocery store, one small and dingy movie theater that showed mostly old westerns, a newspaper office, a small, locally owned clothing store—and the five-and-dime.

When I was a child, the five-and-dime stood like a bastion of wonders from the outside world. Going to the store was a ritual, a reward, an experience, and an education all rolled into one trip. It was, of course, not open on Sunday. And, for all I knew, it may or may not have ever opened on weekdays. All I knew about were the Saturdays, when Mother gave us ten cents and allowed us to walk the four or five blocks to the store.

The shopping experience started on the sidewalk in front of the five-and-dime. There were usually a few items like wagons, tubs, mops, and brooms on the way into the store. And there were windows on either side of the wood-and-glass door so you could get a preview of things to come. The excitement started to build.

Immediately upon opening the door, you could smell a wondrous aroma that smacked of the glories within. Years later I realized that smell was probably coming from the oiled wooden floors. The floors were kept clean by sweeping fresh sawdust over them once a week to "attract" the dust. The process left the store with the sweet smell of wood. To me it represented the whole outside world brought within blocks of my home.

Two aisles led from the front door through to the back door, shotgun style. There were flattop counters on both sides of each aisle, about eyeball height for a child. The counters nearest the door had little glass compartments filled with trinkets, jewelry, little dolls, cars, books, folding fans, perfume, and every other wonderful thing you could imagine. And, best of all, the items really did cost five cents, ten cents, and sometimes two-for-five cents. No Mattel toys, no fancy packaging, no plastic, and no brand names. Just wondrous trinkets that opened new doors of imagination and play.

Down the aisle from the trinkets were the sewing notions—buttons, thread, needles, bias tape—and six or nine bolts of cloth. The sewing notions were very important because that is usually what got us in the store in the first place. Mother would need thread for a sewing project, and we all got to go with her to the store.

The interior was dark by today's standards. Glitzy displays of merchandise had yet to be invented. What you saw at first glance was it. But that was enough. A true, heartfelt shopper was born in those sweet-smelling wooden aisles.

It seems quaint that ten cents could be considered a shopping spree. But life was very different then. Daily life centered on home and family, not going and schedules. Schools were nearby, churches were nearby, and there was no commute time to anywhere. Challenges consisted of how to get homogenized milk trucked into our little grocery store before it "went bad."

Nobody ever considered that life was boring or that we longed for bigger and better things. The local five-and-dime had everything we needed, on two aisles.

When life gets hectic and time crunches threaten to run my nerves ragged, or when we're almost late to church because of the twenty-five-minute drive, I close my eyes and remember simpler times. I don't want to go back, I just want to keep on track with the memories.

Look to the Wise Women of Age

After all, it is those who have a deep and real inner life who are best able to deal with the irritating details of outer life. —EVELYN UNDERHILL

A favorite Sunday morning ritual in many churches is a baby dedication. The new baby and his or her happy family are presented to the church with our promises of prayer and spiritual support. The new mom and dad stand so proud, praying that the baby doesn't make a fuss and disrupt the service. The congregation all stretch and peer around heads to catch a good look at the sweet baby. The pastor is in all his glory, bestowing the Lord's blessings on this new life and the young family. It's a special time in the life of a loving and caring church.

Something like this happened to Mary and Joseph and Baby Jesus. When Jesus was about a month old, the Holy Family went to the Temple, according to an ancient tradition of the Jewish faith. Mary and Joseph offered their sacrifices—a lamb of the first year and a young pigeon—as the Scripture specified. Mary's days of purification were fulfilled.

At the Temple the family encountered a prophetess, Anna, who had been widowed at a young age and had spent her long life as a part of the resident staff. Possibly Anna did not have any sons or other male relatives to support her after her husband died, so she devoted herself to prayer, fasting, and praise in the Temple. As the years went by, age and experience bore heavy on Anna, and she was given a divine gift of understanding future events.

Anna was, no doubt, well-versed in the knowledge of the Law and the Prophets and looked forward to the coming of the promised Messiah. When Anna saw the family with the Baby Jesus, she knew in her heart she had seen the living God. "And coming in that instant she gave thanks to the Lord, and spoke of Him to all those who looked for redemption in Jerusalem" (Luke 2:38).

Call it age, call it experience, call it divine intervention, call it intuition, call it astute awareness—there are wise women of age who *know* things. When you have lived a long time and have carefully observed the intricacies of human nature year after year, when you have prayed diligently and trusted the Lord through many circumstances, there comes an eerie, uncanny ability to know things. It is a gift of age—an awesome gift.

This gift can go unrecognized when it is used in the wrong ways. It can take on the appearance of meddling, bragging, passing judgment, and predicting more than was revealed. In these cases, wise women of age become a nuisance to their families and are no longer good to the Kingdom.

Anna used her gift for good. She recognized the Messiah and simply gave praise for having been a participant in this sighting and understanding.

Likewise, true wise women of age use the gift only in accordance with the will of God, and only as truth is revealed. They tout no irrational miracles. The gift is used sparingly and carefully guarded, not to be flamboyant or call attention to oneself.

These wise women of age are stable thinkers, they sustain happiness through all of life's trials, they have a heightened consciousness, and they find and proclaim the world to be unspeakably beautiful. Wise women tell time by eternity, not by watches and calendars.

If you live wisely and if you live long, you can acquire membership in this most esteemed group. But bear in mind that living a magic number of years will not be enough to assure your status. The years must be lived in a particular way, a way fitting for a sage or a wise woman of age. The trials must be handled as growth, not as defeat. The successes must be shared and the love always turned outward in service.

A wise woman of age does not have all the answers, but she now knows what questions to ask. She celebrates each moment in the near presence of God. She realizes that wisdom, understanding, and life experiences are all gifts from a loving God—gifts that must be given back to the world.

By the time Mary and Joseph brought their newborn son to the Temple, they should have been accustomed to wonderful and strange events. It had only been a few short weeks since they had been a part of the most celebrated event ever staged in human time: heavenly hosts singing glory to God, shepherds showing up unexpectedly, a bright star in the East, and all the holiness God could send down. So encountering Anna was probably not that unusual for them.

But in today's world, we need to watch carefully for the wonders of God's revelation in daily life. Look for wise women of age. They may have a message.

THANKSGIVING

Our works of charity are nothing but the overflow of our love of God from within.— MOTHER TERESA

When our young adult mission team got back from Antigua, the most important impression was the gratitude of the people of the island. Even though they lived in the worst of poverty conditions, the people spent much time being thankful for what they had. Most of the homes—bare huts with no electricity or plumbing—had been partially destroyed by a hurricane more than a year earlier. As the months passed there was no money or materials or labor to have the homes repaired. The gaping holes just turned into bigger gaping holes. Yet the people were happy and grateful for what they did have. They continued to thank God for the rain, even though it soaked their homes through the destroyed roofs. They thanked God for their one meager meal of the day. And they thanked God for the Americans who came to help rebuild their homes.

In contrast, I look at my own living conditions here at this Thanksgiving season. My roof is solid with no leaks, no big holes for rain to pour through. My bathrooms are clean, with scrubbed white tile and hot-and-cold running water at my fingertips.

The table is heavy, abundant with delectable dishes—more food than we can eat in a week. Christmas gifts are already accumulating in one corner of the living room. Another extravagant holiday is on the way.

Do these luxuries escape me? Do I constantly realize how very blessed we are? When deep-felt gratitude is missing, we miss out on more than we realize.

Remember the Bible story describing how Jesus restored ten lepers to health? Nine healed men went their way and never looked back. Only one man did not take his newfound health for granted. He returned to Jesus to express his gratitude. And remember Jesus' question, "But where are the nine?"

Can you imagine being miraculously healed from a social and medical disaster and then walking off without a backward glance?

I wonder how many times I may have overlooked a gift, a miracle, or a joyful surprise and forgotten to be thankful. Maybe I just added the blessing to all my others and went merrily on my way. And in the process I missed the near presence of God.

Let your Thanksgiving season be full of holy and sincere gratitude, constant in the awareness of the goodness of God.

Rejoice in the Lord always. Again I will say, rejoice! Philippians 4:4

TEARS

The soul would have no rainbows
If the eyes had no tears. —BARBARA JOHNSON

My husband likes to gleefully tell anyone who will listen, "Suzanne is such a crier, she can even manage to cry at supermarket openings." And it's true. I have a very quick tear reflex—at least that's how I refer to it.

I can watch any two beings (animals, humans, friends, enemies—it doesn't matter) in a scene where one is saying good-bye to the other, and I will cry every single time. A television commercial recently showed a mother watching her young child get on a school bus and ride off to the first day of school. I cried every time it played. It was just so sweet to see their relationship and see the loneliness as they separated.

Happiness always sets me off too. My brother and sister-in-law shared their good fortune with our family by giving us a generous sum of money when his business stock went public. Was I happy? I cried until I couldn't cry anymore. It was so warmhearted of the two of them to do that. We were so happy that crying was the only response that came to me.

Of course, I do an outstanding job of sad tears. When someone suggests going to a movie, my first question is, "Does it have any sad parts?" I do myself and everyone else a huge favor by staying out of sad movies. As a child, *Bambi* scarred me for life. I had the hard sobs for days. I finally worked up my courage to see *The Lion King* video in my own home; I had to fast-forward through the sad parts.

I have noticed that both my husband and my sons use my tears vicariously. Since they grew up with the notion that "real men don't cry," they have to have some way to show sadness. Many times they have looked at me in a tearful situation and said, almost hopefully, "Mom, are you going to cry?"

But I have now learned that tears are nothing to be ashamed of. In fact, I am rather proud that I can feel so deeply about things. And, more important, people who know how to cry also are the people who know how to laugh. The self-control that shields a person from tears is the same control that secures the emotions against being open to laughter.

I can't speak for everyone who cries, but for me tears come from a well of joy deep within my being. Not always happiness, but genuine joy. Happiness is something people invented—a happy day, a happy event. But joy is something very different. Joy comes from God. Joy is such a wonderful surprise welling up so unexpectedly, it just makes me cry.

Tears are a vital cleansing element in a woman's life. It helps you know you are still alive and in true touch with your deep well of joy.

WHY?

Every child born into the world is a new thought of God, an ever fresh and radiant possibility.

—KATE DOUGLAS WIGGIN

The condition of human suffering has long been debated in Christian circles. And when the suffering falls on a tiny child, it makes even less sense to people who believe in a loving God.

Do I believe God willed that my precious baby girl would suffer just so He could teach us more about His love? And when our friends told us they felt Sara had been born to the "right" parents, were they explaining away a choice they felt God had made? Were they saying that God consciously decided to "reward" our family with a handicapped child?

Not in a billion, jillion years could I believe that! The God I love and trust does not send trouble.

It is never the will of God for anyone to suffer. God does not cause suffering, and He does not make little children grow up in bodies that are broken and weak. Sometimes adults bring pain and suffering on themselves by disobeying the rules of nature and not caring for themselves and their physical bodies. Sometimes human carelessness causes pain and suffering, as in automobile accidents. And sometimes living in a finite and imperfect world results in illness and suffering. Our bodies interact with many influences, both genetic and environmental. Mortality is a fact of life. But none of these things reflect God's justice, as I understand it.

How then can a loving Creator allow us to live in a world where we daily face cancer, death, disease, fear, and pain? Time after time we have all been a part of a caring group that has prayed long and hard for a cure or a recovery, only to have ultimately lost the battle and experienced illness and death anyway. How can this be?

Does God have a weekly quota of illnesses to distribute and selectively bestow on the people "most likely to succeed"?

I can never believe that! Instead, I feel the world is set up in a way in which both good and evil are at work. Both wellness and sickness exist. Both sadness and happiness are available for our taking. Pain is a natural part of life. Germs, viruses, and malignant tumors are a part of the real world. When we are alive in an imperfect world, we have to take all the good and bad together. Life is not fair. And *this* is where the love of God comes in.

Through the grace of our loving God, we can move beyond the question of "Why?" and move instead to the question of "What do I do with what I have been given?" This is the meaning of being human, created in the image of God. We are free to make positive choices that can take a very bad situation and turn it into an opportunity for experiencing His grace, His strength, His presence, and His love.

Suffering *can* help us explore the limits of our capacity for knowing God; it leads us to discover our own depths of perseverance and strength. As we begin to see our tragedy in the context of a mostly good life, we can begin to know God.

The love of God exists in its strongest and purest form in the very midst of suffering and tragedy. We do not love God because He protects us from all sorrow and all harm. We love Him because loving Him makes us better and stronger in sorrow and pain. We love Him because He is the source of our hope and courage in an imperfect world.

God did not cause Sara's disability. It happened because we live in a world of imperfection and defects. But His infinite mercy has led us hour by hour, day by day, month by month to new depths of coping. God works with us where we are and helps us move toward where we can be.

JUST NOD YES

Raising children requires courage, not to mention a sense of humor. —LIZ CURTIS HIGGS

A housepainter was busy painting the wood trim on our house. During the four-day job, three-year-old Jason took it on himself to be the official family host for "the nice painter man." Jason followed him from door to window to window, visiting and watching the work progress. I offered repeatedly to occupy Jason's interest elsewhere, but the painter insisted the audience was fine. He said he enjoyed the company.

I knew that few people could comprehend Jason's three-year-old chatter, so I offered a little advice. "If you don't understand what he's saying, just nod and say 'uh huh.' It will be less trouble than trying to understand what the words are."

The painter looked at me in horror. "No ma'am," he said. "From the look in that child's eyes, I would never give him an affirmative answer without fully understanding every word I was agreeing to."

Smart painter man!

Then he said, "Lady, how do *you* understand what he is saying?"

I was Jason's mother, that's how I understood him. For the most part, I had taught him every word he used. I was there when he learned the words. I was there when he put two and three words together to make a sentence. I knew how his little mind worked. I knew what kind of sequence he thought in. I just knew his language patterns in a way that no one else did.

To me, that is a good illustration of how God knows us. Even when our conversation is somewhat unintelligible, God knows what we are saying because He has been fully centered and fully focused on us from the beginning.

Jesus used this kind of focus when He was on earth. He looked at people in a way that saw their earliest beginnings and their deepest longings. I can imagine that Jesus had deep, penetrating eyes that connected His focus to the other person.

People responded to Jesus because of this intense connection. He understood their message of need and then responded with His message of hope. Jesus *knew* what they were saying.

This same connection needs to be a part of our encounters as well. It takes time and undivided attention to understand another person, but the payoff is amazing. Focus fully on the person to whom you are talking. Read the body language. Watch for the tone of voice. Does it match the words? Look for the comfort level of the person talking—nervous and jittery? Angry? Relaxed? Frustrated? What is the tone of the conversation?

When you unequivocally listen with your eyes and ears and intuition, you will come away with a complete message.

Concentrate on people.

SUCCESSFUL SELLER OF PURPLE

There is a transcendent power in example. We reform others unconsciously when we walk uprightly. —ANNE SOPHIE SWETCHINE

After the Resurrection, Jesus continued to appear in a new and transformed image to His disciples and followers. For about six weeks there were recorded sightings and encounters. Jesus' altered presence continued to stretch the minds of the believers in a way that they understood more and more of what Jesus had been teaching. The message took roots and grew.

The disciples began to move outward into villages and towns, into the countryside and even out into other countries and continents—just as Jesus had commanded.

Several women continued to be a part of this missionary endeavor. Women in the New Testament were not sideline spectators when it came to Jesus' ministry. As the zeal was catching on and expanding, they continued to work side by side in ministry with the men. Some of the women may have been present with Jesus as He taught the crowds and healed the sick. Other women joined that group along the way as new converts to the persuasive power that seemed to surround the traveling apostles. No doubt, these women then became supporters of the new Christian communities as they were established.

When Paul crossed the water into Macedonia, he came to the culturally advanced city of Philippi, a Roman colony. Paul preached and many converts joined the movement.

Tradition holds that the first convert on European soil was an impressive, career-minded woman named Lydia, who was highly successful in her own right. Lydia sold purple dyes, one of the costliest products of her time. Only the very rich, such as Roman officials and nobility, could afford fabrics dyed in purple. This gave Lydia connections in high places, as well as considerable wealth of her own.

I have always loved purple. I am thankful that this magnificent color is now affordable for all of us to enjoy. In my early adult years, I had a lovely Bible teacher who made Lydia come to life for us—and to this day I think of the Bible's high-end saleslady every time I wear something purple.

I like to think that Lydia had one of the grandest homes in town. I can see her entertaining and being a gracious hostess to all the city's elite. This would be the entrepreneurial way. Philippi was very unlike Palestine, where women were regarded as chattel. The women of Philippi enjoyed great independence and were free to gather in public places; they ran their own businesses and were big players in the drama of the early church.

Lydia and the other townspeople met at the riverbank regularly to pray and listen to speakers tell them more about God. When Paul came to town, Lydia organized such large and enthusiastic public gatherings that they annoyed the Roman authorities. The soldiers broke up the crowds and put Paul in jail. When he was released by a converted jailer, Lydia was there to take Paul into her home to treat his injuries and care for him in safety.

Lydia was a Spirit-empowered woman, a recognized community leader, hardworking, bold, and intelligent. She worked tirelessly to help the cause of Christ. No doubt she supported the ministry of Paul, long after he left Philippi, with gifts of money, time, and influence.

What a natural way for women to get involved in service. Lydia speaks to us even today, challenging businesswomen—women who have the means to give significant gifts and women who have influence—to use these special abilities to the glory of God.

Her example of generosity opened doors for countless generations of believers to know the living Lord. Her total commitment to the mission of the gospel is felt two thousand years later as we recall this gracious hostess and talented organizer. How I would love to know that something I do today will be felt by believers two thousand years from now.

Go Looking for Trouble

> *If you don't like the way the world is, you change it. You have an obligation to change it. You just do it one step at a time.*
>
> —Marian Wright Edelman

When you live in a city, you don't have to look far to see impoverished areas that house enough human tragedy to keep you awake nights for the rest of your life. And if you don't see it as you drive through the city streets, all you have to do is listen to the local news on TV. Stories of bleak faces, tormented and demented minds, hungry children in desperate environments. Older citizens stuck in decaying, filthy rooms barely able to take care of themselves. Homeless women and children living on the streets. And the circumstances go on and on.

In a land where most people have so much, how can some people have so little?

To *see* human need is to *answer* human need. To follow Christ is to embrace the ugliness and neediness of the human family and to say, "How can I help?"

Let me tell you how—*get involved!* If you want happiness, if you want an escape from loneliness and poor self-esteem, if you want true joy, if you want to know the fullness of God's love, then get involved in healing human suffering.

There are nonprofit agencies throughout your town that work every day in this human-need arena. These agencies always have a volunteer program that offers opportunities for people like you to come along. Or you can go to a local school and offer your services.

Babies and children in the hospital need loving attention. Older citizens need meals. Children need warm coats. Teens need encouragement from a big sister. Mothers need rides to the doctor or the grocery store. Frail seniors need a friend and someone to talk to. International students need English teachers. Just where can you best fit in?

I had a call this very week from one of my seniors who has been active in the center for many years. Now she is homebound with complications from a broken hip. She called to get names and phone numbers of other homebound seniors so she could call and cheer them up. "I have a lot of time on my hands," she said, "and I just thought I could use that time to make life good for another lonely senior."

Most of us are quick to agree that "they" need to do something about the crime and violence in our cities. But what are *you* doing about it? True, one person can't fix much. But, by the grace of God, *everyone* can do something to make the city and the world a better place for at least one other person.

Blessed are those who do not turn away from the struggles and needs of the human race. Blessed are the ones who go forward spreading God's love throughout their streets, the city, and the world.

ONE STEP AT A TIME

My precious family and friends have taught me that joy and sorrow, storms and sunshine, tears and laughter are all part of living—and the sun does shine on the other side. —MARGARET JENSEN

When Sara was born, the knowledge that I had an unlimited supply of sustaining, comforting resources did not lessen the pain we felt as we watched our baby cry through endless hours. Many times we stood by her little bed in the hospital and touched or held her as the pain racked her frail little body for days and nights on end. There were times I fell to the floor in exhaustion. Her unrelenting pain sucked the very life out of me.

Sara had major fractures about every six months. In between times, we handled her like a china doll. We carried her on a little mattress cradled in our arms. We were reluctant to let other people handle her, for fear of more fractures. So we couldn't use a baby-sitter or leave her in the nursery at church.

Sara's sunny disposition filled our good days with laughter and smiles and precious little sounds. How she loved her big brothers! She loved watching their antics and loved their attention to her.

The constant fear of more painful fractures hovered over our home like a great storm cloud. We could hardly enjoy the good times for dreading the bad times. The fear became as big as the pain.

At times I was very angry at God for not taking this tragedy away. In my frustration and fatigue I had to blame someone. My anger was intense and violent. How could this suffering continue? I was afraid dealing with the pain would overwhelm our family, our marriage, and my own health. Anguish and heartbreak wore me down on more than one occasion.

How could we go on? This was a long-term problem, not one that would go away in a week or so. Where could we find the physical strength to continue?

I prayed. Oh, how I prayed. I read Isaiah 40:31. "But those who wait on the LORD/Shall renew their strength;/They shall mount up with wings like eagles,/They shall run and not be weary,/They shall walk and not faint."

I thought about soaring like an eagle and quickly ruled that out as a possibility. Then I considered running without getting tired. I didn't think I could do that either. Gladly I would settle now for walking and not feeling faint. Maybe I could do that, just until noon.

Until noon! Until bedtime! Just for today! I had finally hit on a coping plan: one step at a time. All I had to do was make it just until noon. I could help that sweet baby feel better and comfort two frazzled little boys—just until noon. At noon I could put up another span of time and do what was needed—just until six o'clock. I made it through each day by focusing on small segments of time. It is amazing how much strength it takes to carry the thought of tomorrow. And how much easier it is to deal with just today, or just half of today.

Sometimes I think spiritual and physical strength is like manna: you get just what you need for the day, no more.

Conquering Fear

You have to go through being scared before you can be brave. —SARA EZELL, AGE SEVEN

Sara knows a lot about fear. We have spent many hours in emergency rooms, in doctor's offices, and in treatment rooms. These locations fabricate fear. They not only give life to fear but cultivate it and grow it into consuming proportions. What will the doctor want to try next? What sorts of pain and discomfort lurk just outside the next opening of the door? What kind of time line can we put on this fearful experience? A week in the hospital? Six weeks in a cast? Two hours of waiting for X-rays?

We developed an array of coping mechanisms to deal with the debilitating fear spawned by broken legs and arms. As we waited we told favorite stories or made up stories about the people we saw around us. Sometimes we began naming all the good things we had going for us at the moment. We prayed a lot. And as an icing-on-the-cake activity, we planned a surprise for ourselves at the end of the ordeal—a family vacation, a new toy, a trip to the ice cream store for a big fluffy shake or a hot fudge sundae.

Mostly we learned to walk right up to fear, shake hands, and then move on. We know now that once you go through true terror and come out on the other side, you really do envision yourself to be very brave.

It's true that sometimes fear is necessary. It protects us from taking dangerous risks. It is a survival signal that warns us of hazards and perils. But I am talking here about the kinds of things nightmares are made of. Cold, immobilizing fear is a terrible feeling in and of itself. However, the fear of fear is even worse. Then we become so terrified by fear that it can suck the very life out of a normal existence. That kind of fear mushrooms into full-blown anxiety and prevents us from enjoying many aspects of life.

We have a friend who is terrified of tornadoes. Even a forecast of widely scattered thundershowers can send him searching for the nearest basement shelter. Roger has never been in a tornado, he has never even seen a tornado, and he has no firsthand knowledge of tornadoes. But he has developed a consuming fear of the *possibility* of a tornado. If only he could reason through his panic, he would realize that his smoking habit has killed more people during one day than tornadoes kill in three years. But fear is not always logical.

Extreme fear is really a danger in itself. Worrying about a car wreck, or having cancer, or getting food poisoning can cause more harmful health problems than some of the diseases we obsess over. And we all agree that *worry never reduces the risk of anything*.

The media feeds our fears like pouring gas on an open flame. Mad cow disease has been described and embellished on TV until we are certain that a tiny bite of beef will instantly send us into writhing fits. Yet there has never been a single case of mad cow disease in the U.S. The fear is vastly overblown.

During one summer week in Nashville, we recorded a senseless murder every single day. Each evening on the six o'clock news we saw body after body being removed from a crime scene. We experienced the tears and anguish of family after family dealing with a horrible loss. By the end of the week, we were almost afraid to leave our homes.

The fact is that while six people did get killed that week, well over one million people in the area did not even get shot at. So while a few precautions may have been helpful, a real fear of being murdered was unfounded.

Fear is like a great wave in the ocean. Once the water starts rolling in, it picks up more water, and nothing can stop it. The wave just keeps on rolling into shore, consuming everything in its path.

If you want to conquer your fears, Sara and I have some suggestions you:

1. **Face your fear head-on.** Discuss your fear with someone. Is it realistic? What is the likelihood of it happening? Can you prevent the thing you are fearful of?
2. **Redirect your fear.** Decide on something very specific that brings you peace—a Bible verse, a song, a thought, a person. Bring this image to your mind over and over. When the fear begins to make its ugly way into your

consciousness, replace the fear with your redirection plan: quote the verse, sing the song, think your positive thoughts as hard as you can for as long as you need to. The fear will slowly begin to shrink in size.

3. **Claim your fear as your own.** You can be saved from many accidents and disasters, but no one can rescue you from your fear except you. Personal fears and anxieties are yours and yours alone. Only you can lay them down.
4. **Be assured of God's presence.** God does not promise an absence of bad things. But He does promise strength in the presence of danger. Trust in God. Move beyond your fear to be brave.

I sought the LORD, and He heard me,
And delivered me from all my fears. Psalm 34:4

Write it out! Did someone really make you mad? Get on your last nerve? Feeling blue, neglected, or lonely? Just grab a pencil and write about it. Tell that little book all about it.

Keep a special notebook close at hand or start a personal "tell all" file on your computer. Then, when you feel like unloading about how unfair life is, flip on that switch and bare your soul.

Don't worry about grammar or spelling. These words are for you alone. But do date each entry, so you can measure your progress later.

Describe the exact situation that caused your stress, then talk about your feelings. You don't need to spend time analyzing your feelings. Just record them.

Think it over. Don't you feel better already?

Friends Who Walk Beside

My special friends, who know me so well and love me anyway, give me daily encouragement to keep on. —EMILIE BARNES

Few journeys are a solitary walk. Even though I cherish my moments alone, I draw the most strength from being with people. Other people nurture me, encourage me, draw me out of my doldrums, and give me courage.

God made us to be social creatures. He created us for sharing, for reaching out, and for drawing close. The most profound meanings in life come in the process of loving and being loved.

Jesus was certainly aware of this social need when He selected twelve men to be His companions throughout His earthy ministry. The Bible records many struggles these friends had in trying to learn and understand the basis for the journey. They often fell short, no doubt causing Jesus to wonder if they would ever get the point. But the accounts of how meaningful the friendships were to Jesus set the standard for us all.

I think about the friends I encounter each day at my senior center, both staff and seniors. If you want a true-blue friend, pick a senior. We start each visit with a big hug, then we get down to business sharing aches and pains, then we move to the good times coming up.

I think of good friends who hold my hand and tell me what a good job I'm doing. I think about my friends who challenge me and nudge me out of my pity party and back into real life. I think of the friends who bring casseroles when I'm sick or a loaf of hot bread when Sara is in a cast. And the friends who call and say, "I was just thinking about you today. How are things?"

I certainly think about the cherished friends in my Sunday school class who sustain each other on a weekly basis. I think about my little friends who bring me drawings, and bugs, and pine cones. I think about my friend who lives miles away; we only talk once or twice a year. But I feel her presence and hold every memory close.

How lonely the Walk would be without my traveling companions. They enrich my steps. They hold me up when the going gets rough and join in my chorus when my skies are blue.

REINVENTING THE WHEEL(S)

You see, the body of a bumblebee is too big, its wingspan too narrow, for it to be able to fly. Yet it flies around doing what God made it to do.

—THELMA L. WELLS

Sara's first spoken word was *go*. We could tell by the happy, expectant look on her face, she knew full well what she was saying. By the age of two, she planned on *going*—any place, any time, for any reason—and the fact that her little legs would not support her was only a minor detail. In fact, when the boys asked me if they could go barefoot, Sara cried and begged to "go" there too! It took a great deal of explaining that "barefoot" was not a place; Sara was fully convinced she was missing out on something.

For short trips around the house, from the toy box to the TV and back, Sara had an elaborate mobility system consisting of rolling and scooting, which was actually quite efficient. When the distance was too far for this method, she asked to "use Daddy's legs." Six-foot-six-inch Mancil would pick her up and take her where she wanted to go.

But we could see that wheels for Sara would become an important and permanent part of our family. The first set of wheels was a little orthopedic walker that completely surrounded Sara so that she was protected on all sides. It took a while for her to learn to use it, but when she did—look out! She was all over that house like a streak of lightning. When she was tired, her older brothers would take turns thrilling her with free rides, wheeling her walker all over the house while I looked on holding my breath. This mode of transportation got Sara to school and church independently, which was new to all of us.

By the third grade Sara needed a bigger and better set of wheels. This was back in the olden days when wheelchairs were hospital-green, one-size-fits-all contraptions. But her new chair had wheels and independent suspension, which greatly excited the boys. Jason, age seven, carefully explained to Sara about independent suspension. "It matches the wheels to the bumps," he said. This pitiful green chair not only elevated Sara to table height, it became a fun new toy. Every minute Sara wasn't using it, the boys were selling rides to other kids.

The chair was a real hit with everyone, except Grandmother. When she came for a visit, she announced that the ugly green chair had to go. "You can do better than that! In Texas I have seen fun, bright-colored chairs. Let's go shopping." Soon a jazzy purple wheelchair came to live with us and Sara loved it. She sat so proud, like a queen riding in her carriage.

But many broken bones later, Sara's arms just wouldn't roll that chair with any dependability. It was time for a new chair with a *motor,* much to the delight of the boys. So "Heidi," named by Sara's best fifth-grade friend, came to live with us. Heidi was tailor-fit to Sara's size and was an instant revolution in her life. Despite its much smaller size, it cost about the same as the boys' first car! And it seemed to me to go just as fast.

Learning to drive the electric wheelchair was an experience we remember well. Mancil was often appalled at the dents and scratches on the furniture and door facings. But Chase and Jason would painstakingly explain to Sara how to navigate, and before long Sara was the Mario Andretti of wheelchairs. Shopping became a popular pastime now that Heidi could take Sara to any store in the mall. School was more fun because Sara could keep up and even surpass the other kids for the first time. Church was easier because she could go to her Sunday school class by herself.

As we reinvented the wheels in Sara's life, we discovered that the tools for independence come in all shapes and sizes. Old chrome walkers, hospital-green, one-size-fits-all chairs, and high-tech Heidis have all filled a need at one time or another. Each was better than the last, and each contributed to Sara's life in a unique way. The next time you see a person in a motorized chair, remember Heidi and thank God for the contribution those wheels have made in that person's life.

HAMBURGERS FOR EVERYONE

Ultimate hatred and ultimate love met on those two crosspieces of wood. Suffering and love were brought into harmony. —ELIZABETH ELLIOT

The year was 1960 and I can still remember the very day it happened. We were on a Baptist Student Union trip to a neighboring college campus. It was a regional conference for all the officers of the BSU. We had the big white van we used for trips. There were seven officers, all of us good friends. We studied together, ate together, and volunteered our time to keep the BSU programs running. Trips were great fun—a weekend of mixing and meeting new students from other campuses.

The trip began about midmorning on a Friday. By noon we were ready to stop for lunch. The driver selected a little roadside cafe; no McDonald's were available then. Everyone quickly climbed out of the van, eager to eat. Well, everyone except Zelda. Zelda just sat there in the van, looking out the window. She didn't say anything.

"Come on, Zelda, let's get some lunch!" someone shouted back toward the van.

All of a sudden the air was electric. The hair on the back of our necks stood out. The realization hit each of us at the same instant: Zelda couldn't come in for lunch. The cafe did not serve blacks.

Two minutes before we were just a happy-go-lucky bunch of college kids out for a good time. In a heartbeat we had each been bolted to reality. There were *cans* and the *cannots* in society. And the line between them was drawn right down the middle of our little group!

As long as we were on campus, the color of Zelda's skin was a nonissue. In fact, I doubt that anyone had even noticed the difference. Zelda was just one of us. Part of the group. Fun to be with. But once we left campus, it became a big issue. Zelda couldn't eat lunch with us, and there wasn't a restroom along the entire length of highway she could use!

Never before in my sheltered, little-town life had I come up against so drastic a realization. In West Texas, I had always gone to segregated schools, churches, and events. Integration was a word that drifted in from the big cities. Occasionally we saw a newscast relating the perils of segregation. But since we had never been face-to-face with the issue of civil rights, we simply had never focused on this dreadful reality. Until now. Until it had happened to one of *us*.

That particular situation ended with one person going into the restaurant and ordering seven hamburgers to go. We all ate in the van.

But the seven people in that van were never the same again. We returned to that campus different people. From that day forward we joined the hundreds of young people across the nation who were beginning to work on putting the terrible injustices and profound sadness of racial bias behind us.

How intolerable to know that much of the same inequity *still* exists thirty years later. As long as any woman, regardless of race or class, lives in fear for her life and the lives of her children, we cannot rest. As long as innocent children grow up in neighborhoods where gunshots interrupt school recess, we must not rest.

Any woman whose spiritual walk does not take her through the troubled waters of injustice and prejudice with a mission to do something about it simply does not understand the Walk.

WHAT ARE FRIENDS FOR?

My mission is to travel globally, extracting diamonds out of people's dust. —THELMA L. WELLS

Five-year-old Skye went off to kindergarten and quickly encountered the ways of the real world—kids acting like grown-ups sometimes do.

Skye and Elizabeth quickly hooked up as "best, best friends" in the classroom. On certain days, Rachel was also included as a third best friend. The school days passed with the two, sometimes three, little girls playing together, going home with one another, eating at McDonald's together, and going to the others' birthday parties. Life was good.

But one day Skye came home in tears, crying as if her heart had broken. Elizabeth had come to school that day and announced that she no longer wanted to be Skye's best, best friend. She and Rachel had talked it over and they wanted to be best, best friends with each other, and they did not want Skye to be their friend anymore.

Rejection! What a crushing blow at any age. Of all the human emotions, rejection must rank right at the top of any list as the worst.

Skye and her wise mother sat down and talked about the situation. They talked about what it meant to be friends with someone. They talked about how bad it hurt when friends treat you badly. And they explored several options of what to do next.

Finally they decided that, at the very least, Elizabeth should know how badly Skye's feelings had been hurt by her decision not to be friends.

So Skye called Elizabeth on the phone and said, "Elizabeth, I'm sorry you decided not to be my friend anymore. It hurt my feelings, because I liked being your friend. But it's OK if you want to be Rachel's friend instead. When you want to be my friend again, I'll be glad to be your friend."

A bigger woman than I. My tendency might have leaned toward a tad of revenge.

Not Skye. She represented what true-blue friendship is all about. This specific friendship may not last a lifetime; it may not even last until junior high. But the lessons Skye learned with this experience will be with her for years to come. And, hopefully, Elizabeth will be able to carry a little of this experience with her too.

Friendships are not always easy. Sometimes friends require more from you than you are willing to give. Sometimes they pull you down like an anchor. These friends have to be taken in small doses and carefully measured times.

Some friends are so instantly on your same wavelength that within minutes you are sure you have known them for years.

Other friends come along and are actually very different from you, but a single shared experience brings you together.

Some of my best friends live so far away, we have to depend on long-distance connections to keep our friendship going. But in between times, our memories and fondness sustain the relationship.

Some friends are best, best, tell-all friends. Some friends are more like acquaintances. These are the ones who are fun for an event but are not good for secrets. And it is really important to know the difference.

Friends are like a quilt with lots of different shapes, sizes, colors, and patterns of fabric. But the end result brings you warmth and comfort in a support system that makes your life richer and fuller.

MAKE YOURSELF *RIGHT* AT HOME

When children become adults, they remember the little things you did together, like playing ball, roasting marshmallows, or hiking a trail. They rarely remember toys. —BARBARA JENKINS

Have you ever watched a baby bird learning to fly? Or a child learning to walk? They venture out just a little, then return to safety. Next time they venture a little farther, then wait for a perceived danger, and again return quickly to safety.

Home is like that. I was surprised at how hard it was—for all of us—when it was time for our twenty-one or twenty-three or twenty-five-year-old babies to leave the nest. After the turbulent teenage years, I sort of dreamed of the departure with an entire celestial choir singing the "Hallelujah Chorus," both for the young adult and for the remaining family.

But it wasn't happy, it was sad. And it took a lot of departures before we got it right. They kept coming back. Somehow reentering the nest, just for short time, reminded all of us why they left in the first place.

And I was glad they felt the need to come back for nurture every once in a while. To me it showed the strong family bonds we had developed through the years. They came home to "right" themselves before experiencing more of the challenges of the big world.

It's hard to grow up and leave home. It must be one of life's most traumatic challenges, this transition from being a child with overzealous parents to being a young, responsible, self-sufficient adult.

I felt really gratified when a darling, young-adult friend of ours, whom we had known since her birth, came to live in Nashville. She was working in a doctoral program at Vanderbilt. Her goals were high, her achievements were high, and the pressures were high. Pretty soon she ran out of coping power and called, in tears, to see if she could come "home" for a little while to *right* herself. It was too far to get to her family in another state. I was glad we had a warm, comforting spot for her to nestle into.

We didn't do anything. She didn't do anything. We just all sat together in the den, talking casually, watching TV. She stayed for three or four days. One afternoon she announced she was feeling better and thought she would go back to her apartment. She had make herself *right* at home.

When the mountains were too high, and the valleys were too low, and the challenges were too intense, I returned again and again to the shelter of my family's home. Something about my old room, my old bed, Mother's cooking, and Daddy's conversation soothed my fears and bandaged my wounds. Just being there made things right.

UNCHANGED MELODY

The more we learn to receive and depend upon His grace in deepening measure, the less anxious we will be about what the future holds.

—CYNTHIA HEALD

There was a big, full-color photo and a full-column story in the Sunday newspaper. Bud Johnson was retiring from the metro bus company. But that wasn't the story. The noteworthiness of the event was that he had been with company all his working career and had driven the same bus route—*for thirty-five years!*

The newspaper reporter thought that was wonderful and wrote about how all the people on the route loved him.

I thought it was the saddest story I had ever read. Thirty-five years. That is 12,775 days exactly alike. No variety. No change. Given, say, ten routes per day, that is 127,750 times over the exact same route! Can you imagine? Well, I guess you could make a point for stability. But a life with no changes from day to day is a sobering thought.

Change is good. Change is necessary. Change brings new life and new opportunities. Change leads you into ways you were not expecting. Change can be growth. Change keeps you from dying bit by bit. Embrace change!

Change comes in two ways. Sometimes you decide you need a change, and you make the choice to move on. Sometimes fate hands you a change you weren't expecting. Both kinds of change are hard in different ways.

Change that you decide to make gives you time to consider all the options and alternatives on the front end—new job, new boss, new place to live, new marital status, whatever. On the front end of this change decision, there obviously has to be a catalyst that shows life not to be what you wanted it to be—poor pay, being passed over for promotion, unsatisfactory working conditions, unresolvable conflict.

At first it's like a trapeze artist trying to jump off the platform to catch the swing. You think and think about how to hold onto the past in some way and just make a few adjustments.

Obviously that doesn't work for long, so you have to move to additional actions—learning to let go, then turning your full attention to the new. And that's where change gets scary. For a moment in time, you are suspended in midair between past and future. This is when you find out what stuff you're made of.

The other kind of traumatic change is the kind that is thrust on you from a secondary source: your job is downsized, your husband walks out, you face a catastrophic illness. Now you're in a quick-change mode where a new plan has to be made in a hurry—no time to think or evaluate. Big life transitions come whether we're ready or not.

First, pick yourself up, dust yourself off, and take a step. Sure, you're scared. Sure, you feel unprepared to go on. You are uncertain where your best resources are. Fear is OK. But standing still and whining only intensifies fear. *Take a step.* Move in some direction.

Second, sudden change sometimes moves you in a direction that turns out better than you ever imagined. Let unexpected changes bring you some things you really wanted—a new part of the country, new friends, a new profession. Since everything is up in the air anyway, throw in the changes you would like to see happen.

Third, make lemonade. I keep an oil painting of a lemon hanging in my kitchen to remind me to make lemonade when life hands me a sack full of lemons. Somehow, get a positive slant on the situation—not an easy thing, I know. But if you can see a tiny piece of the change that has a positive slant, you can begin to build on that.

Fourth, embrace the change. It is a part of your life now, whether you wanted it or not. Resistance to change takes a lot of energy and prevents you from moving on to enjoy life. Yes, I said *enjoy* life. Move on and grow up.

Pray for guidance. Remember, you are still measuring life with a very short stick. God is measuring your life by eternity. He knows how this experience fits into the total picture. Trust Him.

I have had a lot of changes in my life—some shocking, some sad, some planned, and some where I went kicking and screaming every step of the way. But something good has come out of every change. As I bend into the pain of transition, I find myself growing stronger and able to do things I never thought I could do. And most of the time I was able to understand that, yes, the change left me in a more favorable situation than before.

At least it was a hundred times better than driving the same bus route for 12,775 days!

GOOD LESSONS FROM GOOD KIDS

Being a full-time mother is one of the highest salaried jobs in my field, since the payment is pure love. —MILDRED B. VERMONT

Kids are cute, smart, even brilliant at times. Their fresh focus on life's adventures is like a glimpse into the divine. Watching a child play can teach you more about life than any high-priced seminar package. I absolutely cherish the moments I can recall when my children were caught in the act of being darling, all the while teaching me valuable lessons about life. For example:

Enjoy every moment of your life. When our boys were ages three and six, they embarked on the task of digging a hole to China. They selected a shady spot down by the creek, where the soil was soft. Since we preferred a natural landscape, the digging posed no threat to our yard. Every morning the boys could hardly wait to get out of bed, dress, eat their little bowls of Cheerios, and head out to "work."

They each had a shovel taller than they were. From sunup to sundown the boys dug in that hole; they dug without ceasing. They laughed, pretended various games, and continued digging. Sometimes they played with cars and trucks in the hole, building roads and bridges. Through the weeks and months, the hole became deep enough that both boys could sit down in it and not be seen from the kitchen window. They could hide from imaginary beasts.

They never found China, but they did find endless days of satisfying fun. I can remember watching them, feeling all warm and successful inside at having such precious little boys, and thinking, *I hope I can remember to always approach tasks with that kind of enjoyment.*

Enjoy learning at any age. One Sunday during a family lunch, our three children were trying to impress each other with what they were learning in school. Sara went first and said, "Do you know what I've learned in first grade? That your heart is approximately as big as your fist."

Jason went next. "Well, do you know what I've learned in the fourth grade? That your heart is more in the center of your body than way over to one side." Everyone looked at Jason and nodded approval at this newfound knowledge.

Chase topped the conversation off. "Y'all know what I've learned in seventh grade? That girls are *much* better looking than when I was in the first or fourth grades."

True learning can take place at every age of life, and it doesn't have to be in the curriculum plan.

Rejoice in each new day. Be truly thankful for the opportunity to wake up and live. Sara taught me early on how to rejoice in the morning. She loved life better than any little child could, which was surprising given the many trips she made to the hospital with broken bones. But once the pain was subdued, even six weeks in a traction frame could not daunt her spirits. She rejoiced in each new day, and her happiness spilled over to everyone she met.

One morning very early, while it was still dark and the whole household was sleeping, Sara called me into her bedroom.

"Mother," she said, "I just wanted to remind you to wake me up in time. I don't want to miss today!"

This is the day the LORD has made;
We will rejoice and be glad in it. Psalm 118:24

Reaching Back

After all is said and done, relationships are truly the only things that really matter. —LEE EZELL

When I dream dreams of peace and comfort, the scene is always set in Mama Dear's house, the white brick house on 17th Street in Lubbock. It's the house with all the violets near the curb in the front and the sweet peas climbing up the garage wall in the back.

Mama Dear was my grandmother. I gave her that name when I was too young to even remember. It just seemed like such a perfect grandmother name. Everyone thought so, and pretty much everyone called her that.

Since our family moved from town to town in the frequent rotation of pulpits and preachers, Mama Dear's house offered the one real constant in my life. We visited her often, and I usually stayed extra weeks or days with her when school schedules permitted.

Mama Dear was a liberated woman long before the term was ever coined. She owned her own business—The Vogue, an exclusive ladies' ready-to-wear store on the main street in town. She dressed the finest ladies in town for the best events.

To say we were special to each other would only give a glimpse of the truth. Mama Dear not only gave me roots, she spoiled me. She bought me special goodies like little fur coats and fancy dresses. She called me Snookums. She let me play with her makeup and high heels and try on her big hats with feathers. She let me eat—or not eat—anything I wanted. We took the train "to market" to buy new merchandise for her store.

Mama Dear taught me to sew. We spent hours together making doll dresses with lots of rickrack. She taught me how to cut patterns to fit each doll, and I sat at the old Singer sewing machine with my little legs hardly reaching the pedal. Mama Dear said I did a dandy job! I still have those doll dresses and get them out on remembering days to touch and reach back.

Her love for me was unconditional. Mama Dear always had time for me, was always glad to see me, and was always proud of everything I did. At my wedding she sobbed so loudly the guests could hear her all over the church.

As the years passed, we became separated by 1,300 miles. But the ties of the spirit remained forever strong. Eventually circumstances with Mama Dear's health required her to live in a nursing facility, and our visits became even farther apart.

I spend a lot of time now reaching back and picking up the good times we shared, one by one. I spend time compiling scrapbooks and stories about Mama Dear. I am fortunate to have so many things that belonged to her—the beautiful English bone china we use for every special event, the little ceramic praying angel, a brass candlestick, small pieces of costume jewelry, her president's pin from the Business and Professional Women's Club, and many wonderful photos that reinforce the warm and wonderful memories.

Mama Dear is so much a part of who I am. When I feel sad, I know she would make it feel better. When I have good things to share, her memory is there to rejoice. The secrets we shared are still as fresh and special as the days we invented them. In remembering her, I have carried something of who she is with me on my daily journeys. As long as I can remember her walk, smell her perfume, and hear her voice, she will never really be gone.

This year I was lucky enough to find sweet pea plants to start my own vines.

Spend time reaching back into your past. Pull out happy memories and caring people. Know that these people are so much of who you are today. Roots nurture your very soul. Keeping in touch with these roots helps you grow ever stronger.

A Tuesday Full of Hope

Without a purpose larger than oneself, a woman will be empty inside. —BARBARA JENKINS

One morning on the *Today* show, the news announcer reviewed the negotiations for the release of prisoners in Iran. He gave the details, which seemed promising, and then said, "This is a Tuesday full of hope!"

Whoever heard of Tuesdays having hope? Sundays, maybe. Even Mondays might have a little hope. Weekends? Sure. Weekends almost always have hope. But nothing really hopeful ever happens on Tuesdays.

Unless, of course, you *expect* hope on Tuesdays.

So I tried looking for hope on Tuesdays. I would wake up on Tuesday and say to myself, "Today is a Tuesday full of hope!" I would repeat the promise over and over as I dressed and left for the day's activities. I put a lot of feeling into the phrase, like I really expected *hope* to happen. I left the house believing there would be bright hope for all I did that day.

What actually happened was that I created an environment that supported and encouraged hopeful situations. And, with hope, came joy.

I can't begin to tell you what those Tuesdays were like! My Tuesdays were something I looked forward to each week. I started scheduling my most difficult meetings and appointments on Tuesdays because I knew the chances were good that things would go well.

The world is filled with wonder and mystery. We are surrounded every day by so many beautiful surprises. But without hope, we tend to pass right by without even a glance.

On the other hand, we also encounter fear, anxiety, worry, and threats of personal defeat. But I found that all of these encounters pale in the face of hope. Fear and hope cannot coexist.

Share my Tuesdays full of hope! Walk in the new light of godly expectation.

LIVING IN LUXURY

You may be very smart, but a high IQ will not teach you how to live. —BARBARA JENKINS

Engage in a little fantasy. Suppose you had an entire day with no responsibility, no schedule, no demands on your time or energy. For an entire day, you could put yourself in the lap of luxury. What would the day look like? What is your most defined sense of pleasure?

Maybe a long walk in the woods where you lose all sense of time, walking in the sheer pleasure of good health and stamina.

Maybe a day at the spa with attendants catering to your every whim.

Maybe time alone with your love, enjoying the luxury of uninterrupted pleasure, communicating, appreciating the companionship.

Maybe an entire day to wander in and out of antique shops with whatever money you need to buy whatever you want.

Maybe a day at home alone just enjoying your own company. That would be a luxury.

So now, I ask: is luxury all about money? Expensive places and things? In some ways, yes. It takes money to buy some leisure activities. A day at the spa is not cheap. But luxury may be more about time, relationships, and experiences.

Luxury is a condition of abundance, something that provides pleasure but is not absolutely necessary, a sumptuous environment. It may be a place in your home to spend quiet times with all your favorite things around you. Time to enjoy the Sunday paper, good health, personal strength, beautiful memories, an afternoon nap, sleeping late, a clock your grandmother gave you, one daisy in a blue bottle—all are luxuries. All are things that make life extra nice, that provide pleasure. Little things that add up to luxury.

So is luxury something you can buy? Not always. More often, luxury is making the most of what you have.

MIND-BODY CONNECTION

Your world is as big as you make it.
I know, for I used to abide
In the narrowest nest in a corner,
My wings pressing close to my side.

—GEORGIA DOUGLAS JOHNSON

To tell the truth, I get a little nervous with this talk about mind-body connection. Recent research indicates that my state of mind my be a significant factor in my body's ability to ward off illness. The people who write about this phenomenon state that stress is a key factor in staying healthy.

I'm dead before we even get past the first paragraph. I have a type-A personality. I'm the national poster child for stress. I make stress, I thrive on stress. Adrenaline is my drug of choice.

My doctor suggests, on a routine basis, that I enroll in stress-reduction workshops. He even sends me to stress-reduction therapy. But those workshops stress me out so much, I usually don't return for the second session. And those little stress machines they use to demonstrate tenseness—the ones that beep when your muscles tense up—almost short-circuit when I am wired up to them.

Mostly, my stress stems from just wanting to accomplish too many goals. I see an opportunity, and I get involved. For me, controlling stress involves *redirecting* stress, not eliminating it. So I have worked, in connection with good counseling, on a set of checks and balances that help me enjoy my positive stress and manage my negative stress. I'll pass these along to all the stress junkies who enjoy their little adrenaline cocktails.

1. **Pay attention to your body.** It will tell you when stress levels are too high. I have a built-in stress alert: headaches. The minute my negative stress levels begin to build, I can feel the back of my neck tighten and pain shoots up the right side of my head. Those mind-body signals give me the ability to notice and respond to internal stress. Everyone has a stress sensor built into the body somewhere. These overloaded stress sensors are what keep doctors in business.
2. **Face the situation head-on.** If redirecting the stress is not possible, sometimes you just

have to look at the problem, fix what you can, and work around what you can't fix.

3. **It is not the huge problems that cause the most stress.** We usually handle the big problems with finesse and move on with a nice sense of accomplishment. It is the constant single drip of an emotional faucet that eventually wears a person down into a stress attack.
4. **Remain in control of your life.** Anytime you have to be in a martyr role or a victim role, it is putting undue stress on your body.
5. **Stop and focus on the needs of another person.** The higher the stress level, the more important this becomes. Helping someone else, whether it is cooking a meal or making a phone call, benefits your mind and body.
6. **Concentrate on creating a kind and loving relationship with yourself.** Be good to yourself. You don't have to endure high levels of stress unless you want to. Set your limits and stick to them.
7. **Work with a counselor to determine the root cause of your stress.** Sometimes what seems to be the stress is only a symptom. The real stress may be coming from a hidden source you are not even aware of.
8. **Trust God to help you.** He created you to live life to its fullest. It is not His intention for you to self-destruct on overload. He loves you and wants only good health for you. Include Him in your mind-body connection.

HOLY, HOLY, HOLY

Women can splash the world with the love of Christ . . . through kindness, caring, touching, meeting needs, and telling of their love for Christ.

—ESTHER BURROUGHS

Life is holy. Our days, our hours, our minutes are holy, created by God according to His holy purpose. The Bible begins with a beautiful, poetic account of how and what God created. He made a special place. He made it self-contained and filled it with His wonders. Then He gave male and female dominion over it all.

God loved the world and all the creatures He put here. In fact, He loved it so much, He decided to come and dwell here, to walk among the people, to dwell in the countrysides and to visit the lakes and mountains. In Christ He reclaimed the world as a place of fulfillment and transcendence. God revealed Himself in the ordinary: He chose human life as His dwelling place. His presence and His purpose put us on holy ground.

What does that mean? *God is with us.* In the hubbub of our lives, God is with us—in the deadlines, in the splendor, in the singing of a bird, in the frustration of a broken relationship, in the sound of a little voice calling for Mom, in the plumbing repair, in a friend's phone call. He is there in it all; He is present with us. He opens doors for us to love one another, for us to experience peace and beauty. He opens doors for us to enjoy life, to laugh, to find ourselves, and to experience His very holiness, to experience the abundant life.

There's more! God came into this world to summon us to commitment of making life holy for others. What God has done for you, you must now go and do for others. The lonely, the oppressed, the victims—all are waiting for us to live out our holiness. This is not to be confused with a casual twenty-dollar donation to a charity of our choice. It is not the same as the clucking of our tongues when we read sad newspaper stories. It is not even a perfect attendance on the Sunday school class roll.

Making life holy for others requires imagination, sacrifice, courage, empathy, prayer, and perseverance. It is the commitment that does not ask "What's in this for me?" but rather, "If I don't help, what will happen to this life?"

There is no greater joy than bringing light to someone's darkness. There is no greater happiness and satisfaction than lightening someone's burden. There is nothing so holy as being a part of God's touching a broken spirit and creating a new beginning. There is nothing that increases our strength like sharing it with the weak.

Life on earth is the dwelling place of the most holy God. If we are to experience the divine, we must find it in the ordinary walk of each day. We find God in the process of passing His holiness along.

HEROINES OF THE CLASSROOM

Gifts of grace can seldom be understood or explained, only accepted with a grateful heart, a few blessed tears, and open arms. —DEBRA KLINGSPORN

Everyone needs a hero. We certainly did as it came time for us to consider how Sara could go to school. This was before federal laws were passed that ensured public education for all children. Our state law had been passed, but as with many laws, it was not funded. We had an uphill battle.

Sara loved other children, she loved playing, and she was a voracious learner. At age three she could read the TV schedule out of the newspaper. She demonstrated a great love for books and reading and all kinds of learning. Of course, she had two expert tutors at home who taught her things every day. Those two big brothers filled her in on the important knowledge of the world—like cars and trucks, anything with motors, bugs, dogs, turtles— you know, the *good* stuff.

But we knew there was more to be learned. Somehow Sara *would* go to school with the other children! We had a lovely elementary school within a mile of our house. Both boys went to school there, and I wanted Sara there. We found a little walker Sara could use, with a design that helped protect her from accidents or falling. So being with other children was not dangerous.

I contacted the Special Education coordinator and we sat down to talk. To say I was not met with open arms would be a real understatement. I could have enrolled a live cobra with less trouble. Sara would be the first child to be "mainstreamed" into the regular classrooms. The administration personnel looked at me like they could hardly believe what I intended.

Page limitations will not allow the whole story to be told here. As a brief summary, I will just say that Sara *did* go to school. I spent hours of time behind the scenes fixing things, maneuvering situations, and trying to see that things ran smoothly. I learned a lot of tricks on how to work with different school administrators to get what we needed.

We took one year at a time and "fixed" the situation the best we could, given what we had to work with. We praised God for the good years and prayed for mercy during the bad years. And in between we fit in the broken arms and legs.

Sure, some teachers did everything in their power to make Sara feel different—left out—and to make her school experience difficult. The joke was on them, however. Sara loved school anyway.

In the midst of the struggle, we found our heroes, or heroines, as the case may be. And there were many. Sara had teachers who were incredible. They saw a child who loved to learn, who loved all of life. They saw a child who was bright and loving and added to the classroom in a positive way.

Some of the heroines include favorite teachers like Mrs. Peggy Hobbs and Ms. Bessie Fortenberry; they made our lives sing. They rescued Sara from a difficult first-grade teacher, so Sara completed two years in one and still was ahead of the learning curve. These teachers made sure that Sara participated in every school play along with the other children. There wasn't a dry eye in the house when Sara read her Valentine's Day poem on stage.

Then there was a P.E. heroine named Mrs. Helen Smith, who single-handedly created situations that included Sara in games and activities at recess. It took time for her to make a few extra arrangements. But the end result showed all the children that exceptions were all right and that making allowances made life good for all children.

And there was Miss Wynette Sparkman, a heroine for Sara's mind and confidence. She was a first-year teacher of gifted children who never blinked an eye when Sara was placed in her program. She had Sara writing plays, acting in plays, going on TV, and playing educational games that enriched her learning and her self-esteem.

And the high school English and history teacher, Ms. Mary Katherine Bradshaw, who was a heroine for many reasons. She enabled Sara to go on a class trip to Washington, D.C., taking her on the subway, to museums, and through the halls of Congress. She involved Sara in a study of local government at our state capitol. She also was a friend and ally who made routine visits to bring Sara things to occupy her time and mind as she lay at home with a broken leg. These are only a few of the heroines we encountered. You can see that what made them heroic were not life-threatening feats or death-defying tricks. They were simple, everyday actions and ways of thinking that were extraordinary to us.

Because of these heroines, school was a happy, successful place from Sara's viewpoint. She loved every second of her time in a classroom, and when the day was over, she came home to her own classroom at home. She lined her stuffed animals up in neat little rows, set her chalkboard up at the front of the class, got her grade book, and those "children" learned everything she had learned during the day. A love of learning and a love of teaching come so naturally to Sara.

I feel very proud today of what we were able to accomplish in the school system. But it was not without struggles and triumphs along the way. The classroom heroines were invaluable to our success back then, and they encouraged Sara to become a heroine herself. And they may not even know it.

What can you do to be a heroine in someone's life? You may already be one!

STRESS BUSTER

Listen to music. I use symphonic music, usually some of the classics—Bach or Mozart. I keep the tapes in my car, in my office, and at home. Select your very favorite style of music, turn it on loud enough that it really captures your focus. Close your eyes (unless you're driving, of course) and let the music pour over your body like warm honey. Feel yourself lifting with the high notes and falling into the low notes. Totally focus your attention on the instruments, the notes, the mood of the music.

Let the music consume your whole self. Feel the tension falling away from your arms, your neck and your back. After a few total music experiences like this, just the power of suggestion with the same music will begin to feel relaxing.

AN EASTER GIFT OF MY OWN

Even the most tragic happenings will be turned into good for those who love the Lord and are His children. Our spiritual rearing is moved along by the difficulties we face and the mountains we climb. —DOROTHY KELLEY PATTERSON

Just as we have been given the divine gift of eternal life with God, through the resurrection of Jesus Christ, we have, in the process, been given gifts to make this life significant for all eternity. Each of us has been given a variety of resources for living; recognition of these gifts are our own personal resurrection.

These gifts are more than material possessions—much more. They are mind, body, personality, talent, skills, creativity, initiative, resourcefulness, intuition, expectations, individuality . . . the list goes on. These are Resurrection gifts. They cannot be earned, and they cannot be taken away. They can, however, be enriched, enhanced and used to the fullest for the glory of God.

A born-again Easter woman will want to spend considerable time in discovering and exploring personal gifts. The Bible speaks specifically to the giving of gifts.

> *There are diversities of gifts, but the same Spirit. There are differences of ministries, but the same Lord. And there are diversities of activities, but it is the same God who works all in all. . . . But one and the same Spirit works all these things, distributing to each one individually as He wills.*
>
> 1 Corinthians 12:4–6, 11

In my view, these gifts are given to you for two reasons. One, you are gifted for your own enjoyment. These are tools you can use to make yourself happy—abilities, talents, and resourcefulness given to you for your own personal enjoyment. Isn't it just an overwhelming thought to know that God loved you so much, He gave you special characteristics and qualities to use for enjoying your life to its fullest? Your personal resurrection in Christ frees you to accept these gifts.

The second reason you were gifted by God is to make life good for others. The Bible talks about teaching, healing, preaching, and ministry as personal, spiritual gifts. All of these gifts give pleasure and profound joy to the gifted person and to those who benefit from the gifts.

Gifts come in various forms of talents and abilities and come in various durations. For example, each woman is given core gifts that are basic; they are always available. But at certain times in a woman's life, she is gifted with exceptional abilities to match a specific need coming her way. This gift results in comments like, "I don't know how I got through that! Somehow I had what I needed for the moment." God knows when we need a unique gift of grace or endurance to meet an exceptional challenge.

Gifts can be encouraged and developed, but not acquired. It made no difference whatever that my parents sacrificed to pay for piano lessons and voice lessons and made me sing in the church choir for years on end. I had absolutely *no* musical talent or gift. I have the rhythm sense of a solid brick wall. When the ability is not there, move on to something else.

Gifts can lie dormant for a time. You likely have more gifts than you can ever use. So as you explore new avenues of expression, and as you grow in your spiritual life, you can find new and hidden gifts.

Gifts can become so buried by indifference, selfishness, and unconcern that they are rendered useless. A life out of sync with God's will can weaken a gift. Gifts have to be fed and used.

Gifts are for everyone. I get goosebumps when I hear someone say, "I really don't have any talents. I can't do anything." I always back up a few feet from that person in case God decides to deal with her on the spot. To say that one does not possess gifts, talents, and abilities is to deny Creator God. If you are *unaware* of what your gifts are, get busy and find out.

God made you unique, with special talents and abilities. Which gifts from God do you possess?

How can your special set of gifts be used for your own enjoyment and for the good of others? Only you can answer.

WINNING

Life is like a VCR. If you're constantly moving the fast forward, your days will be a blur. If you're always reaching for rewind, you'll miss some nice surprises. Instead, enjoy life in the play mode, content with each frame that passes before your eyes. —LIZ CURTIS HIGGS

Shortly after Tiger Woods won the Masters golf tournament, a reporter asked him what was next in his life. The reporter was suggesting that after such a big victory at such an early age there might be nothing else to look forward to. No challenges left to keep his interest. What would a twenty-one year old do after he had achieved that level of success?

Tiger replied with an understanding far beyond his years. "Winning never gets old if you are still having fun." How extraordinary for a young man to realize the key ingredient—enjoying life as you go along.

It is at that very point that so many people miss the main idea of success. When winning gets to be more important than enjoying the process, everything is askew; even winning is no longer fun. Winning and enjoyment must go hand in hand.

Success and winning can be defined in a variety of ways. "If only I could get that promotion, I would be so happy." "If only we had children!" "If only we had a larger house." "When I get married . . ." Almost anyone can set a realistic goal, make a plan of achievement, and then win. But few people indeed know how to make winning fun.

Making your sales quota, getting the kids raised, and topping your company's goals are all wonderful, exhilarating milestones. But there has to be more to it. Success can be a short-lived moment if reaching that pinnacle has been the sum total of your life.

The real measure of any successful, winning life is the *process* of that win—the passionate pursuit of excellence just because it is fun! The expression of day-to-day striving toward a goal is what gives our lives meaning.

Perhaps this is why some seemingly successful people are forever running back and forth across the planet trying to find happiness. They thought winning would be all. They won early on. They enjoyed success, maybe even fame and fortune, but then the dream was over. There was nothing else to strive for.

I've tried winning and I've tried losing. I like winning a whole lot better. Winning never gets old. Winning feels good. But winning isn't everything. Enjoy the process.

How to Recognize a Christian

To do good things in the world, first you must know who you are and what gives meaning to your life. —PAULA P. BROWNLEE

Within our city is a richly variegated selection of worship styles. And throughout the country the variety widens to a virtual smorgasbord of choices—high church with formal worship services featuring robed choirs that sing anthems accompanied by pipe organs; emotional evangelistic services with enthusiastic worshipers speaking and shouting in ecstasy; small churches with a handful of sincere and dedicated worshipers; and informal groups that sing choruses to the accompaniment of a guitar. Add to that diversity the street preachers, the social worker–evangelists, the silently worshiping monks, and the TV evangelists who take worship right into the living rooms of the viewers. So how can you identify a true believer?

Some religious groups feel they have the one and only truth. They try to create spiritual look-alikes by insisting that all members think, talk, and act just the same. Some other church groups are so loosely configured they hardly use enough organization to keep the group together.

Even within the same congregation there is diversity in worship. At my church, we have three completely different worship services going on at the same time every Sunday. One we call the traditional service, one is a contemporary service with upbeat music, and one is a language-specific service for Spanish-speaking worshipers. Is one service better than another? Is one service nearer to New Testament teaching?

Is one of these groups more Christian than the others? Has God's truth been revealed to one group while all others are wanna-bes? If one of these groups is the "right" way to worship, we would have to determine that other believers would be "wrong."

The only conclusion we can truthfully draw is that religious expression is personal, nurtured only by a firsthand awareness of God. To worship God means that we believe in the value and uniqueness of each human soul. That is how God created us, and that is how we worship.

The Bible is full of accounts of people who had living encounters with the Holy God. They expressed their worship in a variety of ways. David stands out with songs of praise in response to God's goodness. And so does the singing missionary, Paul, who sat in a jail cell and sang praises.

In today's world, I encounter people daily who express their faith in a wide variety of ways. I first think about two precious ladies in our Day Services program at the Senior Center. They face constant cognitive challenges with their daily living tasks. But one of these ladies can still play the piano, and one still remembers the words of their favorite old gospel songs. The sound of their thin voices fills my soul with joyous praise when I hear them every Monday afternoon in their regularly scheduled singalong. There is not a celestial choir God could call from heaven that would thrill your heart more than these two old warriors of the faith.

Next I think of a young woman I met recently, an ex-convict who is devoting her life to ministry behind prison walls. At a businesswomen's luncheon she invited the two women on either side of her to hold hands in prayer before the meal. I know they were as humbled as I was in that personal expression of worship.

Then there is my dear friend at work who has a personal faith expression very different from mine. Religious expression is so much a part of her life that she is a blessing wherever she goes. One day she found me at my desk, crying because of my sister's illness. She held my hands and asked if she could pray for my sister. There in my office she knelt and prayed, then she wrote Marilee a letter promising to pray with her every day.

And I can't leave out the faithful, trusting friends in my Sunday school class who fill their days and weeks delivering meals to frail seniors, visiting the sick, feeding the tired and ill, donating time and money to international students, and exercising their deep faith in God all over town.

Such a variety of faith expressions, showing that God makes Himself known to each of us in personal ways. God comes to us in special moments—reaching out to us, loving us, teaching us His ways—then releasing us to express our praise and adoration in our own way, in our own place, in our own time.

So how can you recognize a Christian? It's easy. By their sincere expression of their love for God and others.

CLIMBING OUT

If we had no winter, the spring would not be so pleasant; if we did not sometimes taste of adversity, prosperity would not be so welcome.

—ANNE BRADSTREET

There is a deep, dark hole. The depth is beyond imagination. The darkness is so black, it crushes in on your chest until it is difficult to take a breath. The footholds along the side of this deep hole have been worn down with the struggle, making escape virtually impossible. No one can reach you to pull you out. Voices can be heard in the distance, but they seem foggy and far away; their words don't register.

Finally, the will to escape gets sucked into its own black hole within the deep, dark hole. It's just easier to give up. But it hurts so bad to be there. The darkness is unrelenting. The panic of needing to escape ebbs and wanes, but the deepness holds on. The days and weeks go on and on.

Even so, you are expected to continue in a sort of daily routine. People are depending on you for food and help. The thousand-pound weights tied to your arms and legs make movement almost unbearable.

The struggle is so horrible, the pain so consuming. The end never comes. Death seems to be the only way out. Dying would be Easy Street compared to living in the deep, dark hole.

Depression. If you have ever been there, you recognize the description. If you have never been there, give thanks to God every day of your life.

We were in New Mexico on vacation one summer when I fell into the deep hole of depression. Sara had an accident and broke her femur, the large bone in the upper leg. For some wonderful reason, she had not had a broken leg in about ten years. I guess I had grown accustomed to the peace and somewhat trauma-free life we had. A major broken bone jolted us back to reality.

Surprisingly, there was not a pediatric orthopedist in Santa Fe who could help us. An hour's ambulance ride to Albuquerque. Waiting, more X-rays, Sara screaming in pain. That precious little face, screwed up in wrenching pain. Then the decision to put her in a body cast. Pain and screaming beyond belief.

Finally, after hours of the worst nightmare, Sara was released—thirteen hundred miles from home, in a body cast.

Sara had never had a body cast before, and the trauma was excruciating. We decided to just hunker down in the hotel for several days and try to get our wits together and get Sara over the initial shock before we tried to deal with flying home. Besides, we had to learn how on earth to handle a body cast. We had no help, no instruction, no suggestions. Just whatever we could figure out.

The week went by, and we felt like we had enough control over the situation to start home. Again, a horror of situations: changing planes, navigating airports, managing a huge cast in a tiny airplane seat.

Family and friends met us in Nashville, and we were home at last. But our trial had just begun.

In the months to come, we found that the trip home apparently had jarred the bone in such a way that healing was questionable, at best. And the longer Sara stayed in the cast, the more brittle all her other bones would become. It was a downward spiral that had no bottom.

Needless to say, I found myself sitting at the very bottom of that deep, dark hole of depression. I had given all my strength away, and I didn't even have the struggle I needed to fight my way out. I seriously considered dying. I tried to plan how it would happen. The only thing that held me back was that I couldn't leave Sara. I figured the boys and Mancil could manage somehow. But Sara needed me for her very survival.

My only response to anything was crying. I couldn't talk on the telephone. I couldn't leave the house. I cried out to God to save me. But my prayers could not penetrate the depression. The deepness and the darkness of that pit had totally cut me off from any hope, from my faith, and from the outside world.

Finally, I was able to put two coherent thoughts together, and Mancil arranged for me to get professional help. We were able to find a wonderful counselor who slowly and steadily led me out of the hole. It was not an easy journey out, nor was it quick.

But that first tiny sliver of light I began to see was the most gorgeous sight of my entire life. I have briefly visited that hole several times since that first encounter, but never for long and never in the same depth.

Believe me when I say that I have worked very hard at understanding my experience with debilitating depression so that I never have to maneuver that dark hole again. I have found certain criteria that now govern my life in order to prevent a recurrence.

1. **Be as good to yourself as you are to other people.** I am a giver, a people-pleaser, usually overriding any needs or pleasures of my own. When I begin to see that darkness approaching, I know I am dealing with unmet personal needs. I have to stop the world and do some things good for myself.
2. **Walking is my best key to warding off depression.** But it has to be a certain kind of walking. As I walk I try to concentrate on the rhythmic movement of my body. Step, swing, step, swing, legs, arms, legs, arms. I usually think of a little chant that matches the rhythm and repeat it quietly as I go. It helps keep my mind focused on my body. I never time these walks, and I never go for distance or speed. I just relish the moments of comfortable rhythm.
3. **I am quick to go for help now**. When the pressures of daily life start to build, I don't turn my head and hope they will go away. Somehow, when those dark storm clouds start gathering, I know to get help in clearing them out.
4. **I know that depression is an illness and not a blight on my spiritual life.** Depression is not caused by my spiritual life not being up to par. On the contrary, my faith in God is what gives me the strength to eventu-

ally pull through this recurring illness. God does not make my life so complicated; I do that by myself. God does not manufacture many of the pressures I have chosen to live with. God did not create the suffering I have had to watch my child endure. But He does offer the grace and strength I can use to survive. What He and I have to do together is to balance the good with the bad—the darkness with the Light. In my weakness, His strength is made perfect.

Three times I pleaded with the Lord to take it away from me. But he said to me, "My grace is sufficient for you, for my power is made perfect in weakness." Therefore I will boast all the more gladly about my weaknesses, so that Christ's power may rest on me. That is why, for Christ's sake, I delight in weaknesses, in insults, in hardships, in persecutions, in difficulties. For when I am weak, then I am strong.

2 Corinthians 12:8–10 NIV

Fair Rules

To believe in God means that all the rules will be fair and there will be wonderful surprises.

—UGO BETTI

Some years ago there was a nun who took her work of ministry very seriously. In the course of her journey, her spiritual expression teamed up with her outstanding artistic ability to give the world a totally new look at religious teaching. Her bright, playful posters were a true celebration in the religious world at that time, because we had never seen anything like it before.

Sister Mary Corita stood as a one-woman art gallery of joyous jubilee in the faith. I loved her work. It was so upbeat and lively, it spoke to viewers on a number of different levels. The technique was good, the colors were magnificent, and the designs were new and crisp. She often incorporated quotations in her work, some her own and some belonging to others. The results packed a wallop.

One poster in particular really caught my attention. The quote at the top of the page was boldly printed in and around large brown circles. *To believe in God means that all the rules will be fair and there will be wonderful surprises.* I had the poster framed and hung it on my wall. I felt I was in possession of a major spiritual truth: all the rules would be fair!

By the midsummer of my life, circumstances had dealt me enough powerful blows that I was practically reeling. I reread the familiar sentence and cried. How could *anyone* think these rules were fair? There was *nothing* fair about life! I took the poster down and put it facing the wall in the back of a storage closet. My pain was too raw to see how things could ever work out to *fair*.

Years later, I ran across the poster again and considered its impact. Well, OK. I could buy into the wonderful surprises part. Good things did happen from time to time. But I still had a lot of ambivalence about fair rules. If life was fair, why was my daughter sitting in a wheelchair? And why was there so much sadness and pain in the world? Back to the closet again. Facing the wall. I was right. The rules aren't fair!

Now in the Autumn of my life, I again have taken the poster out to consider its message. Are the rules fair? I am struggling to understand. Is there a rule that says my life should be one big party with no fear of pain or sorrow? Is there a rule that says I should have as easy a life as my neighbor seems to be having? Is it fair for me to have to work so hard to earn enough to live on? Is it unfair for some people to live in poverty while some have much wealth? Is it fair that Sister Mary Corita herself died with cancer?

My thinking goes in circles. Maybe I was confused about what the rules are. There were no rules to protect me from sickness, from work, from sadness, or even from tragedy. But there *is* a rule that says:

Surely goodness and mercy shall follow me
All the days of my life;
And I will dwell in the house of the LORD
Forever. Psalm 23:6

There is not a rule that exempts me from fatigue and misdirection. But there *is* a rule that says:

> *Trust in the LORD with all your heart,*
> *And lean not on your own understanding;*
> *In all your ways acknowledge Him,*
> *And He shall direct your paths.*
>
> Proverbs 3:5–6

Perhaps if I had spent more time understanding the rules instead of counting their fairness, I would have grown taller in the faith. But maybe that is what the Autumn of my life is for—continued growth.

Maybe I'll hang the poster where I can look at it now.

GET OVER IT!

Our invisible times of quiet determine the stability of our lives. —ANNE ORTLUND

Without question, my son Chase held the world record for two-year-old temper tantrums. The bigger the audience, the bigger the fit. He screamed, he cried, he turned red and then blue, he kicked and beat the floor with his little fists. It was a spectacular sight.

The books by child-care experts all agree that the only antidote to these public events is to ignore the little darling until the fit runs its course.

Fine with me! Considering Chase's size and strength, ignoring was all I could do anyway. A couple of times I had to move him—rather, drag him—out of harm's way. But beyond that ignoring was certainly my method of choice.

Of course, the stares from the people all around were somewhat difficult to overlook. But since I was in ignore mode anyway, all I had to do was extend my ignore boundaries to include the audience. I would pull out a fingernail file and go to work on a nail or two until it was over.

Once, in the center of Dallas Love Field airport, Chase lay down on the big marble star outlined in the floor. As far as I could tell, that star was located smack in the middle of that airport. Every passenger coming in or going out had to pass by it. Chase did not want to change planes. So he screamed until he was breathless. He banged his head a few times, but being of superior intelligence, he determined that marble was a fairly painful head-banging surface.

Unfortunately, he also performed this fit routine in several toy stores, often in our supermarket, and inside every barbershop in three states. For that reason, we dared not visit any barbershop more than once.

But the temper-tantrum monument goes, hands down, to the one in the middle of the sidewalk in a large outdoor mall in Dallas. We were visiting Grandmother and trying to do a little shopping. The way this was accomplished was that one of us would go into a store and shop while the other would walk up and down the sidewalk with the cute little two year old. Then we would switch off.

It was my turn to be in the store. Chase and Grandmother were having a happy little walk outside. For some reason Chase also was carrying the big ring of car keys—no doubt Grandmother felt the keys might buy us a few extra minutes. In a moment of weakness, Grandmother was focused on a little window shopping. Chase took the keys and expertly inserted one of them into the door lock of a very expensive sports car parked at the curb. The key lodged in the lock and wouldn't come out!

Chase hit the ground screaming and kicking. Grandmother was trying desperately to release the key. By this time, an audience began to gather, thinking someone must be torturing the poor baby. I heard the commotion and came to the rescue as fast as possible, but the nice mall policeman got there first. I could hear my mother trying to explain how her car keys got stuck in an expensive car that didn't belong to her and why this tiny child was prone, facedown on the sidewalk, screaming and turning red.

All I can report is, we were not taken to jail, although I think we would have welcomed the escape.

As a side note here, let me explain that my darling little boy was not being bad, he was simply behaving as a normal two year old. The reason his fits seem to stand out in my memory is that I was a new mom. By the time Jason and Sara came along, I was a seasoned parent, able to simply step over the screaming child on the floor and go on my way.

The really sad thing is that temper fits are not the exclusive property of two year olds, or even sixteen year olds. (I've witnessed a few of those too.) Adults are sometimes temper-fit pitchers. And it is not a pretty sight to witness a fit of jealously, pettiness, or selfishness, a bid for attention, or just disappointment that things didn't go their way.

This sort of immature behavior on the part of an adult is embarrassing, inconsiderate, and offensive. I want to go up and take the person's face in both my hands and say emphatically, "Get over it! Grow up!"

Temper tantrums are hard enough to watch in a two year old, but at least it is in the developmental job description of a toddler. But temper tantrums on the part of an adult are a pathetic sight.

However, if an adult of your acquaintance insists on this type of behavior, the very same game plan will work to perfection: ignore, ignore, ignore. Temper fits are no fun at all without an audience.

A soul occupied with great ideas best performs small duties. —HARRIET MARTINEAU

My children enjoy stories of my "good old days." They think it's so funny to imagine the world without e-mail, without personal computers, without microwave ovens, without cable TV, mini-vans, or shopping malls.

While these bigger and more sophisticated toys have improved life in the workplace and the home, they are just the tip of the iceberg on discoveries and inventions during the last twenty-five to thirty years. Think of the huge strides that have been made in medical science alone. People are alive today because their diseases responded favorably to new medications and new techniques in treatment—all developed in the last two decades.

I could go on for pages listing the new inventions that make our lives better, more efficient, healthier and even more fun. But there is one thing we lack in all the new advancements. One essential ingredient cannot be replaced by technology: *human touch.*

We all need it—the recognition, the care, the love that comes with touch. People draw near to us to feel the translation of the presence of God in a caring touch, a pat, a hug. To be truly human is to need to be with other humans, to be in touch, to care how others feel and to express that care through touch.

Newborn infants who are too sick to be held are often helped by gentle touching of their tiny bodies. When Sara was born, she had a broken arm and a broken leg. She was placed in an incubator until a specialist could get to us to determine what kind of care would be indicated. She stayed for a few days after I left the hospital, never having held my baby. I couldn't endure not being with her, so we stood long hours by that little bed, touching, stroking, feeling her baby-soft skin. I was convinced that my nearness to her and the feel of my hands would let her know she was surrounded with love.

The same mother's touch operated when I got home from spending time with Sara. Two little boys needed reassurance that all was well. Mancil and I stroked their little blond heads and held them close. I rubbed their backs, all the while assuring them of God's love and nearness to us. And their little hugs and pats back to me were vast reservoirs of strength.

Any mother will concur that sick children need lots of touching, no matter what age they are. When Sara is racked with the intense pain of a new fracture, we do a lot of touching. It has to be carefully guided so it doesn't cause more discomfort. But I can feel the healing strength pouring into her pain as I gently touch her face, her arms, her back.

When Marilee, my precious sister, spent day after day suffering through the ravages of surgery and treatment for breast cancer, my mother spent the days stroking her, loving her, rubbing her back. Mother and daughter in close personal touch brought a sense of shared pain that helped ease the burden.

Elderly people are sometimes desperate for human touch. The more frail they become, the less people want to touch them. How sad to get to a place where no one hugs you anymore! Touch gives meaning and hope to tired lives and bodies. Being unwanted and untouched is the worst disease an older person can experience.

I have seen well adults who are carrying big burdens and great sorrows surrender their pain in a tearful hug with a caring friend. The touch of an understanding person made all the difference in their sorrow.

Following Jesus into the needs of human hearts, we learn how to wait beside hurting friends, understanding their pain. We learn to reach out with a helpful, caring touch at the right moments. We journey hand in hand alongside friends and family while they pick up broken hearts, go through valleys of deep darkness, cope with pain, celebrate successes, grow in faith, and know the joy of human kindness.

Creative Honesty

Humor is such a strong weapon, such a strong answer. Women have to make jokes about themselves, laugh about themselves, because they have nothing to lose. —AGNES VARDA

If confession is good for the soul, consider me to be having a very good day, because I am about to confess! I have been dishonest as a parent. That's right, I have not always been 100 percent truthful with my children. And even as I write this confession, I will be spilling some secrets that I have carried in my soul for years. Kids, please forgive me! (As if they didn't already know.)

First it was the gerbils. Then the dog. Then the cat. On top of everything else, it was the balloons. Just one maternal falsehood after another. But, in my defense, I *had* to do it. The children would have revolted against me if they had known the truth.

The pair of gerbils (both female, we were assured!) came to live with us as a result of my being tortured, begged, coerced, and run ragged for days. The famous chant that every boy and girl knows by heart was sung night and day: "But we'll take care of them! You won't have to do a thing, honest." And then my favorite verse: "Mom, everyone else has gerbils (dog, cat, mouse, hamster, fish). We just *have* to get gerbils." And the chant goes on. "Let's just go and *look* at gerbils. We don't have to buy any. Honestly, we'll just look!"

We went, we looked, we bought. Home came the gerbils. The precious children changed the cage sixty-two times the first week, four times the second week, and zilch from that point on.

Soon we all decided that having gerbils was not the fun we thought it would be. Except for me—it was exactly the amount of fun I had expected. So we began to discus how to rid ourselves of the little furry creatures we had grown to smell and love.

At this point, the kids were right about one thing—everyone else did seem to already have gerbils, or so they said. So after thirty phone calls, gifting a friend was ruled out. Even the kindergarten teacher declined. What is the school system coming to?

The final-demise debate went on for several days with no firm conclusion. By now, Mancil was in on the act, offering ultimatums: "It is either me or the gerbils!" To top it off, another miracle of the animal kingdom had occurred, and we now had a large family of gerbils. Things were getting desperate. So I suggested donating the whole family back to the pet shop. This met with whoops and wails of unlimited proportions.

Maybe the devil made me do it. Or maybe the growing smell, or maybe both. I concocted a story that would have made Mother Goose proud and told it to my children. "A woman at work has a grandchild who has been sick. She wants something to cheer up the little darling, and she would be willing to take the whole gerbil family—and even share it with the kids at church on Sundays."

It worked. I drove off to work that day, gerbil cage in tow, with everyone feeling all warm and fuzzy about helping the grandmother. On the way, I just happened to stop by the pet shop and make a nice donation. Hey! I was happy. (Actually, I was ecstatic.) The kids were happy. The pet store owner was *not* happy—but two out of three isn't bad.

Now I know what all the books say. I know what the Bible says. But somehow I just don't think those writers have been put to the ultimate kid test. And the gerbil scenario worked so well, I became a repeat offender. Next there was a cute little puppy that needed a stirring explanation of why he wasn't with us anymore. And then there was the psycho cat that hourly ran and impaled itself onto my leg with all four clawed paws. OK, so, maybe there really isn't a cat psychologist that takes in crazy cats. But the kids didn't know that!

If you think I am a mean, bad, evil mother, I remind you that the statute of limitations has run out on all these creative truths. And, to even things up, I also erred on the side of good. For years Sara always got a beautiful bouquet of roses and/or balloons delivered every birthday with a card reading, "Happy Birthday from Chase and Jason." She was thrilled, and the brothers were off the hook for gifts.

The joke was on me. Sara let that practice continue for years after she discovered the origin of the gift was not the boys. One year she said, "Mom, is Jason going to send balloons this year? If so, I hope he sends them to my dorm room."

It Says So in the Bible

An attitude of gratitude . . . is not dependent upon people or circumstances but rather upon a confident faith in the Lord.

—DOROTHY KELLEY PATTERSON

I'm not quite sure exactly where in the Bible the verse is found, but I am positive that there is a commandment from on high that says, "Always eat supper at 6:00, all together. If you don't, something bad will happen."

You may not remember reading that verse. But I know it's there because my dad, who knew all about the Bible, lived as though that commandment were written in stone.

Every night Mother fixed a full dinner and served it to the five of us at exactly 6:00. Not 5:45 and not 6:15. The only exception to this rule was Sunday nights; then we ate after church.

Saturday night was hamburger-cookout night—rain or shine, hot or cold. The ritual was very specific. Daddy worked on the meat patties for an hour, patting them out just so and cooking them just so on his special-made fire. No one else could touch them, pat them, turn them, or serve them, except him.

The weeknight meals were mostly reserved for family—maybe an occasional guest. But the Saturday night cookouts were open to all who wanted to come.

These meals were the backbone of our family. Since TV wasn't even around at that time, we had no temptation to watch the news while we ate. It was a time for family talk, reflecting on all the activities of the day. Everyone had stories to tell, and for about thirty minutes we sat as a closely knit unit to share our part of the world with others who cared.

When I had my own family, we did the same—for a long as we could manage. I always served supper as near to 6:00 as I could get it to the table. As the teen years began to encroach on this tradition, we had to relax the rules a little. But even then we managed to sit down together three or four times a week. (When the boys got their own cars, it dropped to about twice a week.)

There were times I endured a lot of abuse for sticking to this ritual, but when we look back, everyone agrees they were some of the best times we had.

There were a few restrictions on table conversation: no gross-out subjects, no fighting, and no body-parts talk. Just to humor me, we did point out a few table manners, but I'm not sure how well that took. Mancil insisted that the boys take turns pulling the chair out for me; that was only marginally effective.

With the children gone, I admit that 6:00 dinner hour now can get very lonely. I still cook sometimes, and I still get it on the table at 6:00. But the dinner conversation isn't half as lively.

I refuse to let go of the ritual altogether. I plan big holiday celebration dinners—birthdays, Halloween, Valentine's, and of course Easter and Christmas. These dinner events are as near command performances as I can make them. It means that about ten times a year we all gather around that dinner table one more time, to eat, to talk, to listen, to love each other—to be a *family*.

And everyone wonders why I sit looking at it all with a big smile on my face. It is because feeding my little family around my table is just about the happiest time of my whole mothering career. For just a brief space of time the world seems to stop—the fears, the dangers, the hurts, the distance—everything stops for us to enjoy that warm wonderful feeling of family.

Performance Review

It's not a sin to fail, but it's a sin to do less than your best. —BARBARA JOHNSON

Once a year in our agency, we participate in an annual performance review. Each employee is evaluated as to how well he or she performed on the job during the year. We each have a chance to enumerate our successes and explain the tasks that were unproductive. We have to give an accounting of our time and efforts.

The judgment is fair and honest; both employee and supervisor give input. At the end of the review, we set personal goals for the coming year.

I always love this process. When you get a year's worth of accomplishment down on paper, it looks fantastic. I'm always surprised at how much we have been able to do.

There is a parable Jesus used that relates to a similar evaluation process—except that the stakes in the parable are much higher and the end result is more drastic.

The setting of the parable is dramatic. It is the end of time, and Jesus, as King, is on His throne for the final judgment. Surrounding the throne is a host of angels, and in front of Jesus all the people of the world gather for the ultimate assessment. In that final moment of evaluation, each person's life is measured, the transcript of their days is studied, and the whole truth is at last revealed.

Oh my! Can you imagine? My life has been full of choices—good decisions, and decisions I would rather overlook. I truly have a long list of tasks entitled, "Yet to be accomplished."

Not only will my choices be revealed, but my basic attitude about life, about others, and about God will be opened wide for all to see and know. Most of all, my attitude will be opened for Jesus to judge.

I will not be evaluated on my possessions, my professional achievements, or my social standing. It won't matter what part of the city I live in or how I look in my clothes. I will not even be judged on how religious I am nor how many Bible verses I can quote.

My evaluation will rest on more important issues. I will be measured by the care and concern I have shown to others along the way. The great God of the Universe will look at me and say, "How many people did you help clothe? How many hungry people did you help feed? How many lost and wayward souls did you lead to the Light? How much pain did you ease? How many burdens did you help carry?"

And there, in front of God and all the angels and all the people of the world, I will have to answer for myself. An awesome and sobering thought!

Every time I reread this graphic and striking parable, I am brought to task once again. How many hours in my day are spent on labors that will be counted worthless in the final analysis?

But keep reading! The most astonishing part of this parable is yet to come. The most convincing evidence that we are living in love is that we are totally unaware of it. The best witnesses for Jesus are those who are unequivocally surprised when the spotlight is turned on them and shows them involved in Christlike deeds.

> *Then the righteous will answer Him, saying, "Lord, when did we see You hungry and feed You, or thirsty and give You drink? When did we see You a stranger and take You in, or naked and clothe You? Or when did we see You sick, or in prison, and come to You?" And the King will answer and say to them, "Assuredly, I say to you, inasmuch as you did it to one of the least of these My brethren, you did it to Me."*
>
> Matthew 25:37–40

Jesus said, "When you did it easily, naturally, spontaneously, and generously unto the least of these . . ."

This is the criteria we will be evaluated on—the good we do without ever giving it a second thought. The good we do that is a natural part of our daily walk—in traffic, in line, in the dark, at work, behind closed doors, with our family, at the grocery store, with friends. The evaluation covers it all; it is the final measure of *how* we loved.

One evening about 5:30, I ran into the little sandwich shop near my office. I was on my way from work to an important meeting. I was the only customer in the shop, which was good because I was short on time. As I gave my order, I noticed the young sandwich maker had such a sweet face. She was pleasant, efficient, and ready to help speed me on my way. But her eyes were red and swollen, and tears were running down her cheeks.

I was overwhelmed with empathy and compassion. What was wrong? Did she need a friend? Could I help? I contemplated a conversation.

While I ate and tried to decide what to do, she made a phone call. Then she quickly walked to the door and disappeared into the parking lot.

Opportunity gone! I had hesitated and missed.

That young girl comes to my mind so often. A city teeming with needs and craving a message of love—and I missed a cue. No doubt, my final evaluation will include this missed opportunity. I might have made a difference, but I didn't read the situation quickly enough.

Forgive me, Lord. Give me another chance and help me, as I go, to see the cares of a world in need.

Learning Is Fun

To love your child unconditionally is to determine that no matter what, you will always seek his highest good, not your own. —JAN SILVIOUS

Our middle child, Jason, rose to his feet at the age of thirteen months and heard his own drummer, loud and clear. He began his own march at that time and has never looked back.

Jason has always had his own ideas, made his own plans, and cut his own deals. No wonder he has turned into a world-class salesman.

As good as that sounds, Jason would be the first to admit that the world is really not ready for one who knows his own mind. And be assured that public schools were not a good place for creative thinkers.

Jason sent many a teacher to the medicine cabinet. Exceptions were teachers who were good with kids, who knew their subject matter, and who knew how to teach. Unfortunately, classrooms are not always headed by these wonder individuals.

During Jason's fifth-grade year, he had a student teacher who was wise beyond her years. She apparently understood his situation and temperament right away and set about building a friendship. Jason was so grateful to have a person in authority that he could trust, it turned his year completely around. At the end of the year he wrote Mrs. Dozier a letter. She shared it with us as a classic illustration of the teaching–learning relationship.

The spelling is Jason's own:

Dear Mrs. Dozier,

I want to tell you how much I've injoyed having you as a teacher. I wish you could be my teacher every year I'm in school because you make learning so much fun! Before you came, my school year was the pits, low class, terrible, unberible, cheep, and a night mare. But when you came everything was great!!! You're not harsh, cruel, mean, or anything. You're Great!!! It would take a 25 foot long scrole to say all the things I would like to say. But since this is just a piece of notebook paper out of my 100% junk notebook, it will have to do. So I guess I'll end up saying, have a great summer and..... We all love you very, very, much, (inclouding me!) And a little advice from the brain of one of your students, Learning is fun for anyone if the teacher is fun. So if you teach any more, remember to be nice and fun. Hopefuly I'll see you sometime over the summer.

Your good friend,
Jason Ezell

Teaching is a divine calling. Whether we teach at home, at church, or in a school classroom, transfer of knowledge is a significant undertaking. Jesus, our Great Teacher, set the standard. He taught spiritual truths with empathy and understanding. He taught the hard-to-teach. He taught reluctant learners and disruptive people. But each lesson was delivered in love. Can we do less?

PRAISE HIS HOLY NAME

Give God the praise for any well spent day.

—SUSANNA WESLEY

What separates believers into mediocre Christians and Christians truly enthusiastic about their faith? It is the habit of praising God daily. Such a simple thing.

Somewhere in your daily life, clearly apart from corporate worship, structure a time for praising God. Not asking for anything. Not looking for anything. Not with any other motive except praise. God desires and deserves our praise. But, more important, you need the experience.

When you wake each morning, praise God for another day. When things are very difficult, take time to offer praise for the world, for love, and for shelter from the storm. When times are rushed and stressful, stop and praise God for a life that utilizes all your skills. Then praise God for the wonder of creation, of which you are a tiny part. When good things happen, stop and praise God for His goodness. When you look at your family or see photos of loving friends and family, praise God in a big way.

Praising God reduces your cares, levels your anxieties, and multiplies your blessings.

My Sunday school class and I were discussing the act of praising God recently and discovered some ways we offer praise each day. I was enriched by the meanings and the potential of these praise plans.

1. **Keep a journal of praise.** Every day write down what God has done for you that day. Sometimes, if we are out of the habit of praising God, it takes awhile to recognize God's goodness.
2. **Read a praise psalm every day.** Sometimes read the psalm aloud.
3. **Think about God.** Think of His care, His love, His mercy and grace. You can think about God as you drive in traffic, or at your desk, or as you do household chores.
4. **Be on the lookout for wonders**—a flower, a child, a friend, a wave on the beach, a butterfly. The natural world is so full of praise. See the wonder in things you encounter each day.
5. **Practice good health habits.** Taking care of your body is a way of praising God for the miracle of your wonderful working parts. The fact that your body allows you to go through each day is a miracle that invites praise.
6. **Enjoy life.** God intended an abundant life for us all. Enjoy every minute. It is a way of praising.
7. **Use music to praise God.** Sing great praise hymns. Listen to music. Read words from hymnbooks.
8. **Spend time remembering the many ways God has been loving to you down through the years.** You will praise God with a loud voice when you think of a lifetime of love and care.

Get in touch! Stress is something that affects the whole body, even the skin. You can overcome stress by using any one or more of your five senses, including touch. Babies touch their soft blankets to calm themselves. Grown-ups go for a massage. Whatever the method, add touch to your chill-out list.

Make sure that some of that touch includes another living being. Pets are wonderful stress reducers. Stroking a cat or scratching a dog's ear can ease all kinds of ruffled feelings.

But the best touch of all is a big hug from someone who cares. It's so simple, it almost sounds foolish. At least three hugs a day are absolutely necessary for good mental health. I am lucky to work in a place where hugs are a part of our daily routine. Our senior center has a full-time volunteer greeter at the front door who generously dispenses hugs when needed. So many of the folks who visit our center each day live alone and depend on Miss Gertrude to give that all-important hug. The hugs we use are generally accompanied by words of affirmation and affection. That helps too.

Gratitude is the inspiration of heaven's most melodious anthems. Its fruit is joy in the time of mourning, courage in the day of despondency, security in the hour of loneliness, peace in the midst of battle, and satisfaction in spiritual or physical famine. —DOROTHY KELLEY PATTERSON

Joy is very different from happiness. Happiness is a human emotion that comes as a result of good things in life. Joy is a surprise from heaven. Joy falls on you suddenly from above. It is a spiritual experience.

Mary experienced joy when she was visited by the angel to announce she would be the mother of Jesus: "My soul magnifies the Lord,/And my spirit has rejoiced in God my Savior" (Luke 1:46–47).

Elizabeth had a joy experience when Mary visited her with the good news of a Messiah: "As soon as the voice of your greeting sounded in my ears, the babe leaped in my womb for joy" (Luke 1:44).

The angels sang for joy when they announced the birth of the Christ child: "Glory to God in the highest,/And on earth peace, goodwill toward men" (Luke 2:14).

And this joy being shared was passed on to the shepherds. After they saw the Baby Jesus, they also felt the joy: "Then the shepherds returned, glorifying and praising God" (Luke 2:20).

These people couldn't help themselves. Joy came to them suddenly and burst into their lives in a way that resulted in rejoicing.

Remember when you first realized you would be bringing new life into the world? It was joyful—beyond happiness, beyond a smile; it was a shouting type of joy experience. Remember when pudgy little hands brought you creepy-crawly gifts and then hugged your neck and said, "I love you, Mommy"? Remember looking at your husband across the dinner table and feeling all the love and closeness you share? Remember the prayer time when you were suddenly filled with spontaneous, holy hilarity?

In these moments joy surrounds us and bubbles up through us like a geyser.

When we are among the redeemed of the Lord, when our sins are forgiven, when we are reborn in Christ, there is joy. We can't help ourselves. An inner radiance lights up our faces and permeates our whole being. Life is joyful.

Joy, being different from happiness, is the very thing that stays with us and lightens the load during difficult times. When life is tough and nights are long, joy brings the light.

You will show me the path of life;
In Your presence is fullness of joy;
At Your right hand are pleasures forevermore.

Psalm 16:11

Let there be joy.

AMAZING GRACE

Each person grows not only by her own talents or development of her inner beliefs, but also by what she receives from the persons around her.

—IRIS HABERLI

The old song rang out through the tiny chapel at the funeral home: "When we've been there ten thousand years . . ."

I had heard my daddy sing those words a million times in his strong and authoritative bass voice. I loved hearing him sing "Amazing Grace." Daddy sang it as if he had invented the whole idea of grace. He preached the blessings of grace time and time again. So when the minister sat in our living room and said, in his best funeral-planning voice, "And what songs will we be using?" our quick and unanimous choice was "Amazing Grace."

My family had called a few days earlier, in the middle of the night. "Daddy isn't doing well. You probably need to come." Mancil and I made arrangements for the next flight to Texas.

Daddy had had heart bypass surgery years before, and now the arteries were reclogged. That was before we knew a lot about cholesterol, and Daddy had enjoyed his homemade pimiento cheese sandwiches with gusto—and then ice cream for dessert. Now, after additional complications, his heart just gave up the fight.

I sat for a long time in the chapel that day and reflected on Troy Dale, the minister, and Troy Dale, the daddy. I thought about my own trail of parenting and what gifts he had given me for the Walk.

Why was I able to absorb the jolts and pressures of a young family? How was I able to sit in this chapel and feel the quietness and the sense of well-being? Because much of who Troy Dale was as a person was still very much alive and well in me. He and Mother invested solidly in us, and he left each of us with gifts to use on just such occasions as this.

First is the immeasurable gift of personhood—a sense of who we are as persons. As I look back to my childhood and forward to my continued parenthood, I am convinced that this gift of personhood is the greatest single gift a parent can give a child. On this gift all other values come to rest, and without it all other values are lost.

My father, being a small-town minister, had no fame or fortune to give. There would be no trip to the lawyer's office to read a will. But his gift of personhood has been far more valuable and infinitely more useful than money could ever be. This gift is what writers want to put on paper. It is what psychologists describe to patients. It is the subject of preachers' sermons. It is what rich men want to buy and sick people try to find. I received it as a gift—a treasured gift of a parent's love and understanding.

As a parent my father seemed to "have it all together." His value system was firmly established. He seldom had to stop and debate with himself between right and wrong. We three children never had to wonder where Daddy stood on a subject.

In his strong, self-assured way, Daddy taught us that we, too, had what it took to make things right. He and Mother constantly made us aware that we were each unique, created with special and useful gifts. These gifts were to be used, with God's blessing, to aim toward the highest goals and to reach the highest level we were able to achieve. But we were never expected to be more than we were capable of being.

As I look back, I am sure that one of Daddy's greatest strengths as a parent was his ability to make decisions. He allowed us opportunities to make our own decisions; but when we faltered, when we questioned, or when we got too near the edge, Daddy never hesitated to set the example in the decision-making process. I did not always agree with his decisions nor enjoy living with them, but I certainly got a clear understanding of how to make a decision.

Each member of our family felt respected for who he or she was. Daddy made us feel as though a great honor had been bestowed on each of us to hold membership in such a great and wonderful family. We felt noticed, valued, and genuinely loved.

This is not to say that our family existed in a field of clover. In the small towns where we usually lived, the preacher's family was the constant target of pressure. We had setbacks, blows, various health problems—some of them quite serious. During these times I vividly remember our family drawing close together physically and emotionally.

We would all sit close together in the living room. Daddy or Mother would begin to talk. Quietly, and without great displays of emotion, we were informed of whatever crisis had arisen. During these sessions, Daddy and Mother were absolutely honest with us. They never painted pretty pictures when there weren't any. And they didn't promise things they knew wouldn't come true. We were given the facts and then presented with several solutions.

Then we prayed together. Each child, no matter how young, was expected to make his own petition to God on behalf of the family crisis. And each child was expected to voice an opinion on the solution. As a unit, we found peace and security to face each crisis. It was a one-for-all-and-all-for-one decision. We knew that the same unity that produced the decision would be the power to sustain while living through the crisis.

Another aspect of my gift of personhood is the respect for authority I learned from Daddy. I don't understand how he accomplished it. Daddy was not an authoritarian in a way that *demanded* our allegiance. He simply expected to fill the role of authority in our family, and no one seemed to question this. This unquestioned respect for authority gave me a great feeling of security as a child. Even though I often tested it, I always knew who was in charge.

Alongside this establishment of authority was the business of boundary setting. Daddy drew clear, concise, and well-defined boundaries of behavior. Like the decisions, I didn't always agree with the boundaries nor enjoy living within them; but they were reasonable and broad boundaries, and they were set in a spirit of love and fairness.

Daddy was always gravely disappointed when I chose my activities outside his lines. This parental disappointment was far more instrumental than punishment in keeping my behavior within limits. I ached at the thought of disappointing Daddy or hurting his professional role in the community.

Now I have come to say good-bye to my dad. I will miss him with every fiber of my being. But how thankful I am for the vast legacy he is leaving me. It truly is Amazing Grace that has brought us this far, and it will be grace that will lead us home.

Dear God, thank You for life. And thank You for the kind of life that cannot die. Help me as I pass on this great gift of eternal life and sense of being. How I wish I could tie it up in a neat package with pretty wrappings and give it to my children like a Christmas gift. But now I see it has to be given in small measures—lived out day to day in a love-and-pain process. And they will never know what a gift has been given until they are old enough to look back.

NO TRESPASSING!

The soul of a righteous person is nothing but a paradise, in which, as God tells us, he takes his delight. —ST. TERESA OF AVILA

Suppose you got up one morning and made a large sign that said, *No Trespassing!* And what if you hung that big sign around your neck with a bright-colored ribbon and then proceeded through the day?

In this beautiful fantasy, let's imagine that you have a personal space around you that reaches outward eighteen inches in all directions. With the *No Trespassing* sign, no one can come into your personal space without your permission.

As strange as that sounds, women who constantly have their personal space invaded throughout the day become more agitated, more fatigued, and more depressed than women who exercise some control over their space.

But personal body space is not the only space that gets trampled beyond healthy limits. There is also personal *inner* space. In the blissful, comforting silence of your personal space is where your hidden feelings and thoughts are stored. These are the fears and the hopes that are stuffed down, covered up, and saved until later. Time spent in your inner space will uncover these deep-rooted dimensions and allow you an opportunity to understand and work with them.

The more frantic your comings and goings, the more important this inner space becomes. Women who do not take time to nurture this quiet place within usually succumb to unremitting stress, tension, and worries that can lead to illness and destructive habits. When our lives run on and on, every minute filled with tasks that must be accomplished or plans that have to be made, our personal inner space is invaded and destroyed. Only when we take time to experience the silence can we ever center our beings and focus on our real purpose for living.

We need time alone to perceive how God is at work in our world. In a world that is often upside down with pressures and demands, we need a clear and certain purpose for our lives. We can only connect with that purpose in our silent inner space. We also need quiet time to evaluate our relationships, to determine if life is as meaningful as we intend it to be, and to determine if we are living up to our full potential.

The Bible holds a wealth of examples of people nurturing their personal inner space. Jesus used frequent time-outs to visit His inner space. "Therefore when Jesus perceived that they were about to come and take Him by force to make Him king, He departed again to the mountain by Himself alone" (John 6:15).

Many of the Psalms give rich visualizations to help us focus on an inner space and find our silence.

The LORD is my shepherd; I shall not want.
He makes me to lie down in green pastures;
He leads me beside the still waters.
He restores my soul;
He leads me in the paths of righteousness
For His name's sake. Psalm 23:1–3

Open yourself to the Shepherd until you feel peace beyond understanding in your soul. Put up your sign reading *No Trespassing.* Do not let anyone, any fear, any care, or any need move in on your inner space without your permission.

The Walnut Harvest

Friendships are living organisms at work.
They continue to unfold, change, and emerge.

—BARBARA JENKINS

Twenty-five years ago, when my children were very young, I felt it was best for their developing psyches to have at least one parent at home with them most of the time. Since Mancil's job was the one actually putting food on the table, that eliminated him as a stay-home possibility. And as for me—well, women at that time had *jobs* not *careers*. The difference between a job and a career is the size of the paycheck. If I had paid for child care for the two children we had at that time, assuming I could even find acceptable child care, the paycheck would not have been worth the effort. So I stayed home.

My good friend Sara and I often discussed these dismal facts. The paychecks our young husbands brought home didn't stretch to include fun things or, sometimes, even necessary things. We decided we simply had to take matters into our own hands!

Being highly creative types, we decided to make things to sell. We bought fabric, glue, thread, paint, and various other craft items. We cut, pasted, sewed, and covered every square inch of our tiny houses with finished craft items. With a collection of four preschoolers between us, this was not an easy task. But dogged determination and perseverance were our constant companions, and we had great faith in our potential.

Every few weekends, we would pack up our station wagons, leave the children with the daddies, and head to a crafts fair to sell our wares.

This all-out entrepreneurial effort netted us three things: very messy houses, very hungry husbands (who had time to cook?), and very little income.

As if we were starring in a TV sitcom, Sara and I sat down one day to explore the possibility of a Plan B. Was there any way to add to the family budgets without leaving the children?

Sara came up with a plan. She had read in the newspaper about a company in Franklin (a nearby community) that was buying harvested walnuts. Bingo! We had two walnut trees in our yard and knew where there were several more in a nearby park. Our problems were solved!

We gathered all the children, grabbed a lot of big paper bags and boxes, and off we went to harvest walnuts. Hours and hours of backbreaking work. Many sacks of the dirty, green-shelled nuts. A thirty-minute drive to Franklin. We hauled so many walnuts we couldn't move.

Results? $6.41! How did we know the newspaper ad was for *truckloads* of walnuts? The look on our faces when we got that check must have been movie material.

Failure? Not on your life. It was one of the most positive experiences I can ever remember. A friend and I shared a dream, worked together, then laughed long and hard at our naïveté. It also gave us an experience to enjoy and talk about for years to come. To this day we exchange walnut-related gifts—elaborate shopping bags to hunt walnuts with, gloves for picking up walnuts, things like that. And it gave us a measuring stick to evaluate every moneymaking scheme we've had from that day to this.

My precious walnut-harvesting friend! Later in life we shared another experience—breast cancer. Remembering the walnuts gave us both a lot of courage and more laughs. We knew that the same determination that had netted us $6.41 would be a key factor in overcoming our more grown-up difficulties.

WHO ARE YOU?

When you open your heart to God, it's scary stuff, but it will lead to finding your place in the world and harmony with yourself and others. Have courage to make the journey.

—BARBARA JENKINS

My pastor and his wife attended a large community gathering. Mrs. Pastor was circulating throughout the room, meeting folks and involving herself in polite chitchat with various people. She encountered one gentleman who exchanged introductions with her. When he inquired further as to her identity, she mentioned that her husband was pastor of the Such and Such Church.

His eyes lit up, and he said enthusiastically, "Oh, yes, now I know who you are!"

"No, now you know who my husband is," she said. "You still don't know who I am."

Women are often defined by their relationships—Bob's wife, Betty's mom, Helen's daughter, Mary's sister. And when you run out of family to make identifying associations, there is always your job, church affiliation, neighborhood, state, or size and appearance to define you—i.e. the pretty blonde who wears bright colors.

What tells *you* who you are? Sure, all these roles and associations help pinpoint a certain person. But how do you know who *you* are, beyond these descriptive phrases? In other words, how can you affirm yourself as a person with uniqueness, worth, and significance?

Some friends of mine enjoy tracking down their ancestors to determine a sense of identity. A good, solid pedigree can define a person for generations back.

When my children were young and I was known primarily as Chase's mom, or Jason's mom, or Sara's mom, I used to worry what would happen when they grew up and I no longer used that distinguishing label as frequently. Would I still be a real person? Or would I just disappear from the earth? Would I ever be known just by my own name?

I also had trouble going to large social gatherings with my husband. I noticed that when we were in these groups, men usually introduced themselves and then said, "And this is my wife." Or worse yet, "This is the little woman." No name, no personal identity. Just "my wife." It seemed to me they might just have easily said, "And this is my big toe." It has the same warm feeling. So I requested that Mancil please use my name when we were in a group and an introduction was in order. It worked. I became a real person with value and dignity.

Ask some women who they are, and they will answer by telling you what they do professionally or where they work. And the bigger job they have to report, the more significant they feel.

To be successful and recognized by others helps a woman establish a sense of identity, it's true. In being noticed and loved by family, friends, and acquaintances, your self-esteem is nurtured. But there is more to who you are.

Totally apart from whom you are kin to, apart from your talents and gifts, apart from your employment and achievements, is the mature sense of identity that is *you*. Significantly, this is the *you* made in the image of God. This is the *you* that is loved by God for yourself alone. You are somebody because God loves you. You are special to God just because you're *you*—no other reason is needed. All these other relationships? Just icing on the cake.

Life is intricately and intimately linked with Jesus. In fact, Jesus is life—He said so Himself. So when we look for life worth living, we must look for it not in happy or heartbreaking circumstances, health, or even relationships. Life is in Christ.

—JONI EARECKSON TADA

"He said, 'It is finished!' And bowing His head, He gave up His spirit" (John 19:30). The horrendous crucifixion was over. Final.

Joseph of Arimathea asked permission to take the body. Nicodemus brought a hundred pounds of spices. They prepared the body for burial in Joseph's tomb, wrapping linen strips around the legs and arms. Then a large shroud was fitted down over the body and tied at the neck, the waist, and the ankles. Jesus' body was then lovingly placed in the tomb, facing Jerusalem.

To most of His followers, this was a final act. They believed they would never see Jesus again, never hear His words of healing again, never see His kind looks of compassion and caring. Their pain was deep and full of despair.

The story could have ended there. But it didn't.

Yet speed ahead two thousand years and look around. Is it possible that we live today as if the story really did end there? Even as they wrapped Jesus' body for the grave, do we live as though God is bound and nowhere to be found? Have we left Jesus in the tomb?

We live in an era in which murder and violence are constant ways of life. Marriage vows are broken as easily as they are made. Children and women are abused and neglected with astonishing regularity. Women are caught in the web of poverty and low wages. Even nations cannot live in peace. Roll the stone against that tomb! The story of redemption has obviously ended.

But wait! The tomb is empty. The Resurrection *did* occur. Hope *is* alive. God has rolled away the stone and opened new meaning, new possibilities, and eternal life. Our daily defeat has turned into daily victory. God comes with resurrection power to turn our lives into all that they can be. We are Resurrection women.

Throughout His ministry Jesus deliberately violated codes and laws that restricted women and their place in society. He obviously believed that all barriers to being a free and equal member of the community must be challenged. What lesson, what mission, or what role shall women play in this Resurrection?

Modern society has its share of barriers, separateness, injustice, and closed tombs. The Resurrection simply means that all these obstructions must go. Any obstacle that keeps one human being from achieving all he or she was meant to be must go. Limited horizons and restrictive rules are not a part of the Resurrection message.

From equal employment to affordable housing, to barrier-free schools, to opportunities within church membership, to health care for all children—all obstacles must go!

The motivation for change will come from women who themselves were freed from oppression through Jesus Christ. The solitary woman who knows how and when to set an example of working for a better world can set off a chain reaction of motivating force that can roll away the stone and set the Resurrection story free for all women.

Just as it was two thousand years ago, barriers of arrogance and injustice are set in place to protect and preserve an elite group of citizens who already hold all the cards. What Jesus did for women, women should do for all people who are restricted within barriers.

Every time you open possibilities and expand horizons and create opportunities for another, you ensure the message of the Resurrection.

Someone's Going to Get Hurt

Unconditional love is the kind of love that makes no requirements before extending favor.

—JAN SILVIOUS

Henry Kissinger never called. Madeleine Albright has never called. I think they have missed a real opportunity, because after raising two boys with emerging male egos often in conflict, I would have a lot to offer to a discussion on world peace.

Conflict happened on a daily basis, sometimes more often. It always started with a look—"Mom, make him stop! He's looking at me!"—or a challenge—"Mom, make him move. His toe is on my side." Then it would quickly escalate to accepting the challenge: "Move your foot or I'll move it for you!"

At this point my response usually was, "You boys separate now. Someone's going to get hurt!" I don't know why I said that; it certainly didn't have any influence whatsoever on the boys. But I felt it was a warning handed down to me from generations of mothers before me. It must be in the basic mother's manual. Most mothers I know say that.

Within minutes the confrontation usually—no, always—crescendoed into an all-out war, and the fight continued until one brother retreated in agonizing pain from some unmerciful wound inflicted during the heat of battle.

Why do boys fight? Why do grown-ups fight? How can mature, intelligent people develop conflicts so severe that the end result is a neighborhood squabble, splits in the church, divorced marriages, broken homes, and even murder and war?

I guess if I could answer these questions within this small space, no doubt I would be getting calls from the State Department.

So, at the risk of being simplistic, I will just say that conflict among people is inevitable. It is a part of that whole personal freedom thing. One person's freedom getting in the way of another person's freedoms.

Being human involves relational living, and being together creates differences that must be resolved. In other words, the conflicts and the differences we have with others (husband, wife, brother, sister, neighbor, preacher, friend) are not bad. But the way we handle the conflict is what turns ugly.

Differences of opinion can be healthy, creative, and insightful. Conflicts can result in deeper understandings, new dimensions of friendship, and a greater affirmation for both parties. When conflicts are handled in a constructive way, the process can resolve tensions, release hostility, and remove barriers.

People, and families, who never quarrel live in an unrealistic world. Couples who never have a difference of opinion are swallowing a lot of negative feelings.

I encountered an older gentleman recently who was bragging loudly to a small group of listeners, "My wife and I have been married fifty-three years, and we have never had a single disagreement!"

Is this the picture of a perfect marriage? Or, more likely, a picture of a lot of unresolved conflicts, especially on the part of his wife? It is not possible to live among other human beings and never experience a disagreement.

The Bible has a lot to say about experiencing conflict and resolving authentic human responses.

> *For you, brethren, have been called to liberty [freedom]; only do not use liberty [freedom] as an opportunity for the flesh, but through love serve one another. For all the law is fulfilled in one word, even in this: "You shall love your neighbor as your-*

self." But if you bite and devour one another, beware lest you be consumed by one another!

Galatians 5:13–15

Let me suggest four responses to conflict.

First, acknowledge the conflict and the reasons for it. Swallowing your anger and refusing to deal with a difference leads to a long-smoldering situation that will eat away at your insides for years to come. It is hard to overemphasize this step for women. Women generally have been "culturized" into thinking that *nice* girls don't talk back. Or that *good* wives don't rock the boat. "He's just had a bad day, don't get him more upset."

Granted, all conflict resolution is better done during a calm, private, unhurried time of conversation. But continuing to sweep differences out of sight can consume your relationship.

Second, use "I" messages as much as possible instead of "you" messages. Of all the conflict resolution skills, this one works the best, inflicting the least pain to the other person.

This is how it works: Describe your feelings. "*I* feel very lonely when you spend time not talking to me." "*I* feel like I am being taken for granted." "When *I* have to come home at the end of the work day to do more work at home, while everyone else watches TV, *I* feel that I am being taken advantage of." When you use "I" messages and simply describe your own personal feelings, you have not launched an attack on the other person, and you have not created more conflict that will only escalate the problem.

Third, if conflicts persist, go for help. Find a trusted friend who will help mediate or arbitrate.

Find a counselor, a minister, or some other person who can assist in ironing out the conflict. We know so much about human nature now, and so much is known and understood about conflict resolution. It is possible that the grievances are not as irreconcilable as we thought. We do not have to let the destruction of alienation and brokenness overcome us.

Conflict is like a length of sewing thread or knitting yarn. If you get a big tangle in the thread, you have to stop the project until you get the knot out. Otherwise, it is impossible to keep sewing.

Finally, trust your impasse to the Lord. Sometimes only God and time can heal. Trust the relationship to the power of God's mercy and redeeming love.

WHAT, ME WORRY?

The healthiest way to handle mixed emotions is to accept them. —CATHERINE WALKENSHAW

I am a world-class worrier. When I can't think of anything to worry about (which is very rare), then I worry because I'm not worried! Did you ever sit down and think, "Now wasn't I supposed to be worrying about something?"

Describe a simple family situation to me, and I can give you a list of twelve things to worry about in that situation.

If the kids stayed out too late, I worried about their safety. If they came home early, I worried that they didn't have fun or that they had a disagreement with a friend.

If my husband got a promotion at work, I worried that the new pressure would be too much for him. If he didn't get the promotion, I worried that something was wrong or the bosses didn't like him.

If things weren't going well with my work, I felt calm and secure because I had plenty to worry about. If things were going well, I was terrified with worry about what might go wrong.

And what did my husband and children do during my intense worry episodes? Sleep, play, watch TV, read the paper, go out with friends, and otherwise not give a flying flip about the crisis I had going.

Why did I have to do all the worrying for everyone? Why couldn't someone just buy into the moment for a little while and worry with me?

Probably because I was doing such a darn good job of worrying. And I was obviously getting a lot of bounce out of the package, since I kept on doing it. Plus, I could spot such good things to worry about—little obscure worries hidden within each event, things no one else even noticed.

And besides, my mother taught me to worry. She is also an expert worrier, and somehow I figured it came with the territory. You know—wife, mother, worrier—all part of the same package.

One day, right before I took off like a rocket into the big black hole in space, I decided to *stop* worrying—well, to cut down on worrying. Now it may or may not be a coincidence that I decided to slash my worry schedule at the same time my kids grew up and left home. That fact alone cut my worry time in half.

But I did set about to understand my obsession with worry, so I could make life easier for myself—and perhaps live a few extra years. As I pass these steps along, use what you can, if worry is a big part of your everyday life.

1. **Decide what worry is bad and what concern is healthy.** Bad worry is a type of obsession that gets you nowhere. Bad worry is a one-way street leading nowhere. It concerns a situation you did not create and obviously cannot fix. Bad worry situations are completely beyond your control.

   Healthy concern leaves you with some options, and very possibly options you can take action on. Healthy concern is productive worry, giving you a basis for making decisions that will help the situation.
2. **Set a time limit on worry.** Worry is obsessive and addictive. Worry multiplies worry. Setting a time frame to limit worry breaks the chain reaction. Decide to worry like crazy for one hour, or half a day—whatever amount of time you feel the condition warrants. Explore every horrible thing that could happen. Plan the worst case scenario and play it out for all it's worth. But watch that clock. When your worry time is up, *stop worrying!* You can now clear your guilt, because you have given the problem your best shot.

3. **Get Help.** If your worrying is more than an obsession, if it is something that hangs on and won't go away, go to your minister or a professional counselor and ask for help. Life is too short and too good to ruin with a worry problem that is too difficult to handle alone.

For me worry is such a familiar state that I sink into the trap easily, without even realizing I'm there. Fears and anxieties weigh me down. It takes constant monitoring to keep out of the worry rut.

Look at your worry habits carefully. Worry does not have to be a hopeless path.

EMPTY NEST

Today I have wonderful memories of the laughter we built into the walls of our home and our hearts. Today's experiences are tomorrow's memories, and I thank God I took time to make as many as possible. —BARBARA JOHNSON

For years I had read a myriad of articles about the empty nest syndrome. Mothers and fathers are pictured standing at the door of their home, waving good-bye as the last of the children walk out the door, then feeling overwhelming lonely, even devastated, by the empty house.

To tell you the truth, there were days when I truly, happily anticipated, yes, even yearned for an empty nest. The very prospect energized my days and nights.

Now, let me assure you, no mother on earth could love her children more! I gave every hour of parenting a hundred and ten percent, maybe more. My three children are precious beyond words. They are cute, funny, smart, successful, and a delight to be with. They filled my days with laughter and love and grand times. Even now I would drop anything to go see them or fix a meal for them to come to me.

But it's time for them to go! I've got things to do, and it will be so much easier to accomplish things without a toddler hanging on each leg, or a teenager begging for the car or needing a hem fixed.

I have written many a magazine article while sitting at the glass-top dining table, supervising an Indy 500 matchbox-car race under the table and playing Barbie-in-the-Kitchen to one side.

I have performed many a dinner-hostess duty while nursing a broken arm in Sara's room and playing midwife to a family of gerbils in the boys' room.

I have transacted many a business deal on one phone line while negotiating with a high school principal on a second phone line.

You *can* raise a family and do other things, like a career, at the same time; but you can come off looking and acting a little cuckoo at times.

I always liked that verse in the Bible that says, "For this cause, let a man leave his father and his mother . . ." Leaving is God's plan. Phase One of the family gives the child roots—nurture, values, instruction. Phrase Two gives them wings. It is time to sit back and enjoy what a good job you've done.

Without reservation I can say that I loved every minute—well, *liked* every minute—oh well, make that, *survived* every minute of mothering. But I've got places to go, things to do, people to see, books to write, and a life to live! So good-bye, you sweet things. Let's keep in touch.

ONE WOMAN'S MESSAGE

Mary Magdalene was the very first person to share the gospel . . . a plain, ordinary woman who dared to obey. —SANDY SMITH

It was early morning, at first light, when Mary Magdalene returned to the tomb. Only her abiding faith had sustained her during the previous days.

After the horrifying arrest and crucifixion of her beloved Master, she had remained steadfast at the foot of the cross. Every second of His suffering and agony had been hers as well.

Only one man among the followers, James, had been able to withstand both the fear and the anguish of the crucifixion. Nine of the eleven remaining disciples were hiding in fear, somewhere in Jerusalem.

Peter was in seclusion, suffering with remorse for his threefold denial.

But four women refused to abandon the dying Christ. They watched the mocking, the darkness, and the last breath. Then they followed as His body was carried to the tomb.

The Sabbath must have seemed seven days long. The waiting, the confusion, and the uncertain future without the Master weighed heavily on their minds.

Yet the faithful four returned early Sunday morning to complete the tasks at hand. This time it was to anoint the body of Christ with spices as the last tribute of their love and respect.

So many interesting facts emerge at this point in the story. First, the women seemed to have no fear for their own safety, even through all the men seemed to be immobilized with fear. Second, they had a huge obstacle to overcome (the stone), but they went on their way undeterred, knowing they would eventually have a solution. Third, they were intent on the task at hand. The spices were a part of the burial process, something that needed to be done, and it fell to the women to carry through.

Then came the surprise of the empty tomb and the encounter with the messengers in white.

And next the words that have reverberated through two thousand years, the central fact of the Christian faith. "He is not here; He is risen!"

Jesus chose to make a *woman* the first witness to His resurrection. The most significant message of His mission on earth. A dramatic confirmation of His belief in her commitment and spirituality, a tribute to her faith.

How many times this kind of faith has been repeated throughout time. History books are being rewritten to include the important stories of women and their vital contributions to nations, to families, to churches, and to the mission fields. When the going gets tough, women can be counted on.

Mary proved she was the right person for the job. She believed, she worshiped, and she spread the word. Even though the men had to come and see for themselves, they followed Mary's leading.

Mary was in the right place, at the right time, surviving fear, sorrow, and anguish, to be available for a very important task. I think about Mary when my fatigue sets in or when the going gets rough. I think about her faith that never wavered. Can I be trusted to come through when I am needed?

That Won't Work

It is a blessing when the promises inherited by faith in one generation can be passed on to the next. —RHONDA H. KELLEY

I come from a long line of very strong-willed women. My grandmother, great-grandmother, and several aunts were entrepreneurial career women long before it was common for women to have careers. They owned successful businesses, sold magazines, and worked to support themselves with very little help from the men in their lives.

My mother is also a strong, brave woman who thrives on challenges. I have never seen or heard my mother even suggest that something couldn't be done, or that any job was too difficult, or that a plan wouldn't work. She makes a plan, follows through to the last iota, then sometimes continues to go even beyond, grinding a few noses in the final process.

So it comes naturally for me to follow in these fine footsteps through four generations by being another strong-willed woman. No wimpiness for me.

During the early years of our marriage, my unsuspecting young husband made the mistake of saying, "That won't work" or "You can't do it that way!" It finally became clear to him that those two statements simply set that project in concrete as far as I was concerned. At that moment there was no turning back; it was full steam ahead. And I can assure you, dear reader, that with very few exceptions the project in question was completed to perfection. I had no choice. I had generations of ancestors to answer to.

Strong women intrigue me. I enjoy watching them organize large fund-raisers that make life better for less fortunate individuals. I admire parenting skills that strong women use; they work carefully to empower their children and help them grow strong. I enjoy observing strong women manage and make good business decisions. I envy their abilities to run companies and raise frisky families, all at the same time. The world is a good place because of sensitive, strong women.

But when is strength really a weakness? I have to admit that when it comes to the big decisions of life, trusting God is not my first line of thought. Instinctively I look within myself for answers. I am comfortable depending on my own resourcefulness. But the very foundation of a walk with God is complete trust. This kind of trust reflects the sense of security that comes from having Someone in whom to place total faith. This kind of trust calls for a total commitment of mind, purpose, and being. My strength must come from my faith in God, not the other way around. God is the only One who can keep my life straight and who can reveal the true and good will for my days. He does this for women who trust Him to lead.

How often I make my plans and ask for God's blessing on my plan. Then with jaw set I move ahead thinking that my will is His will. Which finds me, again and again, needing to return to my point of departure and seek His wisdom on the front end of a decision—including Him in all of life.

Trusting God does not make me less of a woman; it doesn't compromise my personality as a strong woman. Depending on Him celebrates the wonderful, miraculous gift He has entrusted to me. Trusting Him *is* my strength.

STRESS BUSTER

Look to the sky. Find a comfortable lounge chair suitable for the outdoors—backyard, patio, balcony, wherever. Block out five to ten minutes, longer if possible, to lie on your back and look at the sky. In daylight, watch the clouds move overhead. In the dark, look at the stars. The sheer expanse of the big sky will fill you with awe. Somehow troubles and cares seem so small by comparison. Take a deep breath and focus on the wonders of God.

AUNT ELSIE DIED TODAY

Each person grows not only by her own talents or development of her inner beliefs, but also by what she receives from the persons around her.

—IRIS HABERLI

Cousin Ann called from West Texas to tell me our mutual Aunt Elsie had just died. This was a significant death for our family. Elsie was the last member of her generation in my father's family. The five other siblings had died one by one in recent years. All were "timely" deaths in that they lived rich, full lives and each lasted to see the Winter of their days.

Elsie was the oldest daughter and clearly the rule maker for the entire clan. Elsie set the pace. She alone said when and where the family celebrated special events. She gave the announcement parties and marked anniversaries. She was the absolute and undisputed *Grand Dame* of Christmas, orchestrating memorable family holiday dinners.

I can remember the first year she called a florist and had a centerpiece delivered for the dining table. We were so impressed. No one had store-bought flowers except for weddings and funerals. To have a florist deliver flowers for Christmas dinner was a luxury beyond our belief.

These touches of the lavish gave Aunt Elsie a certain mystique, which she thrived on. Instead of going to J.C. Penney's and purchasing one-size-fits-all organdy curtains, Elsie had a decorator make custom draperies for each window. She had a car with running boards before anyone else. Later she always drove very clean Cadillacs.

Aunt Elsie had enormous impact on my life. As a young girl I used to study her, watching her every nuance and vowing to become the same. Her life was so well-ordered, every detail in place. Even her closet was perfection, decorated with designer hat boxes and padded, flower-print hangers. She controlled her days, her hours, and her image.

In the case of her death, it, too, was vintage Elsie. I asked Cousin Ann how she died, because even at age ninety-six Elsie was in remarkably good health—clear of mind and still calling all the shots.

"Well, it seems she just decided it was time to die. And she did, according to her own plan."

Aunt Elsie selected her burial dress, complete with jewelry and accessories. She wrote out detailed instructions for her service. She even made out the menu and made arrangements for a family luncheon to follow the funeral service. Then she lay down and simply went to sleep. Full control to the very end.

Except for one thing. It rained the entire day of her funeral.

MOTHERHOOD IN A BOX

It doesn't matter if I'm in a very high spiritual moment with God, when that purple dinosaur comes on TV, my two boys want Mommy to watch with them. —DR. SUZAN D. JOHNSON COOK

There are three big cardboard boxes on the top shelf of the closet in the guest room, one for each of the children who grew up here. In each box is their childhood, as we remember it—baby books, drawings, report cards, notes from teachers, party invitations, birthday cards, school pictures, homework—bits and scraps that tell rich stories from the past.

You know, nothing quite prepares you for motherhood—the responsibility, the hard work, the tough decisions, the fatigue, and the fervent hope that you're getting it right.

And truly nothing equals the sense of relationship, the feel of those little arms around your neck, the sleepy head on your shoulder, the macaroni necklaces, the drawings, the handmade greeting cards with big scrawling letters, "I LOVE YOU, MOM." Oh, the joys and the difficulties! The triumphs and the challenges! A love and a mystery that can never be fully explained.

Watching a child grow is like watching a series of the most wonderful miracles you could hope to see. First steps, first words, first car, first date, first book read without any help, first haircut. And for me, all that times three. What joy!

The trouble is that I was so tired as I enjoyed all these special events, I wasn't able to savor each moment as much as I wanted. That's why the memory boxes have come in handy. I can sit down now at my leisure and relive all these moments. As each child gets older and time moves on, these memory moments become more and more important to me.

My babies are grown now. I don't get macaroni necklaces anymore. I get lovely store-bought gifts that can't compare to the handmade gifts but are given with the same love and thoughtfulness. Now I look at my grown children and marvel at what fine young adults they have become. I am full of awe as I see them mold parts of their lives after what they saw me do and say. I see a part of myself in each of them—surely the highest compliment.

And I'm a stronger person for knowing these three precious people. Our unique relationships and their impact on my life constantly enrich my being.

Each day is a commemoration of our lives together, as seen in three cardboard boxes.

A Sense of Self

My experience, and the experience of people of faith throughout the centuries, is one of a God who meets us in the questions, who honors our seeking, and who created us to be intelligent beings. —DEBRA KLINGSPORN

Ginny is a bright-eyed three year old who enjoys a strong personal sense of self. Ginny is always dressed to perfection when she enters the preschool room every morning. Her dresses are adorable with little feminine touches of rickrack and lace. Her strawberry blonde hair is cut in little wisps around her face, giving her the look of a china doll.

But don't be deceived by looks. Ginny is one tough baby. She has two big brothers and learned early on to stand up for what she wanted. Ginny loves the boy toys as much as the boys do. She often plays with the trucks and the favorite of all—the matchbox racetrack set.

One day she stood at the table playing with the race cars. She had an elaborate game going and was intent on the cars and track. A new little boy stood watching from a distance. He was eager to play but seemed to be weighing his options. After a few minutes Patrick made his move. He had evaluated the situation and decided that his size was greater than Ginny's. Besides, she was just a little girl—not much of a challenge. So he smartly strutted up to Ginny and with both hands reached out and gave her a healthy push away from the table.

With lightning quick motion, Ginny turned on that little boy, lowered her voice, narrowed her eyes, clamped her teeth together, stuck her index finger in his face, and very slowly squeezed each word out between her teeth. "Don't . . . push . . . Ginny!"

That little boy, a good head taller and certainly more muscular, was so surprised, he couldn't believe it. He looked as if he had encountered a beehive. He backed up and very quickly moved to the other side of the room.

Go, Ginny! With a self-image like that and a will to defend, Ginny will never find herself in the position of having to make important compromises just to please someone else. Ginny is well on her way to being her own person, someone who makes her own deals and lives by her own rules.

I love this story and have enjoyed knowing Ginny. She stands as a three-year-old monument of a woman who is willing to risk everything to stand up for herself. Think of what a gift this is going to be when Ginny is a teenager and then a young adult building her values. And what a gift it is at any age to like yourself enough to stand up for yourself.

Play. The most amazing thing I ever learned as an adult is the importance of play. Growing up, I never saw adults playing. I saw lots of hard work, some worrying, some more work—and at best I saw adults falling asleep in front of the TV.

But bowling, fishing, traveling, dancing—never. So the concept of taking time off from work to play was just the strangest idea I had heard.

Somehow I could have bought into the play idea better if I could have *earned* the play time by working twice as hard and then deciding on a leisure activity that plugged in at 3:30 and was over by 4:30, so I could get home in time to start dinner on the dot at 5:00.

A very understanding counselor said that wasn't the way it worked. He suggested I just throw my schedule to the wind, take off one day whether my work was done or not, and just enjoy the day doing only fun things.

I had to try several times before I got the hang of it. At first, all I could manage was thirty minutes sandwiched in between appointments. The next time I tried an hour.

Then one day, on a lark, I turned off my computer and said, "I'll be out for the rest of the day." (No need to add that I would be out *playing*, for heaven's sake.) Then I went to a happily-ever-after movie, got my nails done, and shopped for new shoes.

By the time I got home, I was positively giddy. I had such fun! My stress was defused, my body was relaxed.

Since then I've tried playing again and again. It works every time. I have even taken up a new hobby, just for the fun of it.

Relationship Prayer

Hear, O LORD, and answer me, for I am
poor and needy.
Guard my life, for I am devoted to you.
You are my God; save your servant who
trusts in you.
Have mercy on me, O Lord,
for I call to you all day long.
Bring joy to your servant,
for to you, O Lord, I lift up my soul.
You are kind and forgiving, O Lord,
abounding in love to all who call to you.

—PSALM 86:1–5 NIV

Of all the spiritual disciplines, by far the easiest *and* the most complicated is *prayer.*

How many times I have cried to God in my distress only to feel that my requests fell short of being communicated to Him. At times I have felt foolish and powerless and wondered where I went wrong. Where was God? And how could I get to Him?

Prayer is a process, and learning to pray is something that grows and deepens with practice. We will look at various aspects of prayer throughout the next few pages, but in no way can we explore the fullness of the subject here. Communicating with Deity is an awesome and holy event—something to be studied very seriously and without ceasing.

When I am reflecting on prayer, I like to read the psalm–prayers and see how God's close friends communicated with Him. One of these examples is Psalm 86; take a moment to read it. All the verses in this psalm are equally enriching.

To me the key verse is verse 11:

> *Teach me your way, O LORD,*
> *and I will walk in your truth;*
> *give me an undivided heart,*
> *that I may fear your name.* (NIV)

The concept of this verse changed the entire way I looked at prayer. David asked for God's help in a time of great need. But he asked for God's help on God's terms, in God's truth, based on God's wisdom.

How different that is from many prayers I had offered. I frequently presented God with a long list of things I wanted done and how I wanted those things accomplished. I used a laundry-list approach to prayer. I had figured out what *I* needed and wanted, and I even included lists for the folks around me. And many times I included a time schedule for God to use.

And then I wondered why my "prayers" weren't answered.

Those weren't prayers. Those were wish lists to make my life better or my party bigger. There is a vast difference between wishful thinking and prayer, even though we sometimes use them interchangeably.

When we go to God to talk, we go as friend to friend—to praise, to determine His will and His way for our life circumstances. David asked God to walk with him in truth and to give him an undivided heart so that they could be in close communion.

What a difference in motive! I don't *tell* God what to do! Instead I talk to God in an effort to understand His way and His plan, keeping in mind that God's timetable differs from mine. He doesn't use a watch to determine the hour, He uses eternity to tell time. Prayer is about establishing and maintaining a relationship, not about getting what I want.

I also note that God is all-knowing—about me, my needs, my wants, and my requests. He sees the whole picture and has the long-range plan. My perspective, on the other hand , is limited. My thinking is self-focused and short-sighted in scope.

In the Autumn of my life, I can look back now and see clearly that if God had taken my many wish lists and answered even most of them according to my instructions, my life would be a tangled mess of desires.

For great is your love toward me;
you have delivered my soul from the depths of the grave. Psalm 86:13 NIV

THE PRAYER OF SILENCE

I always begin my prayer in silence, for it is in the silence of the heart that God speaks.

—MOTHER TERESA

A couple of times I have had the misfortune to be sitting before my computer screen, diligently working on a document, when the network jams and the screen goes blank. I sit there in horror and disbelief, staring at that blank screen, thinking that surely I'm dreaming, and, in just a moment, the words will reappear. But no, the document is gone. And since I had not remembered to save it, the document is gone to the obscure land of lost computer words.

Sometimes I have had that same experience with prayer. When everything is going great—no trouble, no crisis—praying is easy. God seems to be sitting right there with me, and we can commune as friend with friend.

But there have been times when such a heavy crisis loomed over my life that my prayer screen seemed to go dark. The blank screen looked back at me in mockery. How frightening! I would feel so very alone and empty. I would try to reach out to God, but it felt like there was no one there. My fear and desperation seemed to short-circuit the prayer connection, and just when I needed God the most, I couldn't find Him.

I don't have a good explanation for why this happens. I think it is because the storm is just crashing so loudly that it drowns out all communication.

So, what to do? Feeling cut off from our power source is a huge crisis for a Christian. How can we get to God? I suspect that each Christian who has faced this crisis has a plan. But I can share my plan and say that this is what works for me.

When my heart is breaking and the darkness surrounds my thoughts, I simply have to wait in silence. Never before has Psalm 46:10 meant so much to me as it does in this situation. "*Be still,* and know that I am God." God already knows my heart, my pain, and my prayer. The Spirit has seen to that. So what I can do is *be still.* I must sit still in the presence of God, whether I can feel Him there or not.

I think the apostle Paul had this same problem in mind when he wrote about it in Romans:

> *In the same way, the Spirit helps us in our weakness. We do not know what we ought to pray, but the Spirit himself intercedes for us with groans that words cannot express. And he who searches our hearts knows the mind of the Spirit, because the Spirit intercedes for the saints in accordance with God's will.* 8:26–27 NIV

What an encouraging promise, to know that God's Spirit broods over our desolation when we cannot pray and responds with understanding and power until we can pray again. Just sit still in the presence of God—no words are necessary.

The second realization that gives me courage during these kinds of times is this: when I find I cannot pray, I can live in trust. Despite the desolation I experience and the desperation that overwhelms me, I can remember other days when things have been different. I try to think about the times when I felt the very nearness of God, when my spirit soared as I walked with the Lord. And, remembering those times, I affirm those peak moments with trust. I try to focus and reclaim the certainties that once centered my faith, knowing that the Spirit is praying for me the prayer that I cannot pray for myself.

Then one day the wonderful moment comes when the storm clouds begin to roll away, when the darkness is once again, slowly, replaced by light, and God's presence breaks through within me again. The Spirit helped me in my weakness and in my darkness. It is a gift.

With all my heart, I believe that the prayers of silence can be the most powerful prayers of all. Just "be still, and know"—and the Spirit does the rest.

Carry Out the Garbage

The biggest handicap in the world is negative thinking. —HEATHER WHITESTONE

One morning I came downstairs to plug in the coffeepot. My eyes were still half shut. My house shoes were sliding along the wood floor, making swishing sounds. I was still trying to think where I was and why was I up at this hour. As I flipped on the lights in the kitchen, I was very much awakened to the moment by a smell that made me want to run for fresh air. Someone forgot to empty the trash last night! Mancil was out of town, so I guess it must have been *me!* No one else to blame. Now I had to do the dirty job and get that stinky garbage out the door quickly. Yuck! I took out the sack and spent the next fifteen minutes wiping the kitchen down with cleanser and spraying room deodorizer.

Later that week I was talking to, or rather listening to, a friend air her troubles. She was railing about her daughter, who wears her skirts too short and doesn't ever stay at home. She was lashing out about her husband, who was working late more and more. She was worried sick about her mother, who didn't have enough to do and was wasting her life away playing bridge every day. She was mad at the president and the local mayor. And on she went.

I was listening and responding occasionally with polite "uh-huhs." Then it dawned on me like a light bulb: this friend had not carried her garbage out! What's more, I think she had failed to carry it out for a long time. And, even worse, Friend was carrying her big, stinky garbage bag along with her—I could smell it and hear it!

The vision of nameless Friend standing there with three or four big sacks of garbage slung over her shoulders brought a smile to my face, but Friend didn't notice because she was well into a list of health problems she was naming. No wonder a bad back was among the list. Carrying that much rotting garbage certainly does put a strain on the back.

Even if something stupendous happened right before her eyes, Friend would miss the whole miracle because she was totally preoccupied with the big sacks of her own emotional trash.

A spiritual life threatened by too much personal garbage. Not only storing up garbage from days and years past, but working at stealing garbage from tomorrow!

What fills those spiritual Hefty bags? Persistent anxiety, nagging worries, deeply rooted grudges, jealously, regrets, missed opportunities, disappointed dreams, nursed grievances, resentments, hostility—just to name a few. No wonder it smells so bad! That adds up to a lot of trash. For heaven's sake, take your garbage out!

Think about the exact pieces of garbage in your bag. Maybe a grudge that has been hanging around for a few years. Maybe some pent-up anger at someone. Write all your garbage down on slips of paper, put them in a garbage bag and *take it out*. Then write letters or make phone calls to set things straight between you and whomever or whatever needs forgiving, forgetting, or loving.

Expert garbage collectors completely miss life's daily miracles, the presence of God's love, and creative moments with the Spirit. Any ultimate hope or significant vision of the kingdom is always sustained by the meaning we find in being fully alive each day. The greatest price that spiritual garbage collectors pay is the loss of the magic of the present moment—the possibilities in today.

Abandon the vendettas. Forsake the rage and pity, whether it is directed at yourself or others.

Don't let chronic misery and gloom rob you of the goodness of today.

Lay the garbage bags down. Trash is heavy and it really smells bad. Enter the present moment and put yourself on alert to the awakenings of the Spirit in the ordinary events of the day. Life will come alive in a way you never thought possible.

LET'S TALK

The most profound fear is the fear of regection.

—DENNIS AND BARBARA RAINEY

Communication is a curious thing. Sometimes communication between two people relies on words. But many times communication requires no words at all.

Babies communicate readily long before they can speak. People who are ill and cannot speak find ways of communicating without words.

Mothers and children have a large repertoire of messages that don't require a single word. Remember the tap on your shoulder during church? Remember the little pinch on your arm? Remember your mom's lowered eyebrows? All of those gestures communicated a world of information without words.

And remember the beginning years of your marriage relationship? Words were rarely necessary. "I love you." "I need you." "Bad day at the office, can I have a little extra TLC?" "If you slam that cabinet door one more time, you're history." All these thoughts can be effectively communicated between two people without a single word.

Then there is the kind of communication in which there are words, but the words and the message don't match. A friend says, "Oh yes, I'm just fine. No problem!" But her voice is high-pitched and pinched, and the look on her face is full of pain.

My husband used to have an expression, "That doesn't bother me! I couldn't care less!" I soon learned that what he really meant was, "I'm hurt and I care more than I want to admit." The words and the message just didn't match.

However, the saddest kind of communication is when the lines have gone dead altogether. All the words are clipped and brief. No nonverbal messages pass between the parties. The eyes no longer belie little secret messages. The two people keep thinking there must be messages somewhere, but instead there is just miscommunication.

At this point, the only hope is to sit down together and use the two words, "Let's talk." And make sure that the message and the words match.

A Big Loss

Christianity does not offer escape from circumstances; it offers conquest of circumstances.

—JAN SILVIOUS

When they called with the diagnosis, we sat stunned, trying to fit the word *cancer* into our family picture. My sister had breast cancer; no one in our family had ever had cancer before.

She lived with her beautiful family in Texas—four wonderful children and a college-professor husband. Marilee was beautiful, loving, outgoing, and a credit to her community. She helped teachers develop strategies for teaching young children with disabilities. Marilee was so gregarious and always a joy to be with. Everywhere she went people knew her and loved her.

We missed being together, separated by so many miles. When summers permitted, our families met in New Mexico, near Santa Fe, and enjoyed Glorietta together. We never realized what cherished times and happy memories we were creating.

Here I was in Tennessee, far from the scene and the pain—no way to offer support. Her family called to let me know what the doctor reported. A guarded optimism. Surgery. A little chemo. Everything should be all right.

But somehow I knew differently. Call it intuition, call it a premonition, call it cold terror. A few nights later, I even had a dream that reinforced the feeling that cancer would take my sister from us.

Marilee had had polio when we were very young. Her future hung in the balance for many months. Her resulting condition was a weakness for back pain. She got sick easily, and somehow I was afraid that this would be her demise.

For two years Marilee battled the cancer with the courage of a warrior. Her faith was enviable. Her sweet family rallied around her, and she had an important support group from all areas of the country praying for her. Marilee endured the harshest kind of chemo reactions. When the cancer won, we were almost joyous that she didn't have to suffer anymore.

The loss was worse than I ever could have imagined. She was so full of life and had so much to give to the world. Now, she was gone. I no longer had a sister. How could a loving God let this happen?

The loss expanded and grew. I not only lost a sister, but for a time I also lost hope, lost courage, and lost faith! In the place of hope I had pain, unrelenting pain. In the place of courage, there was a big gaping fear. How far would this disease go? Was it fair for me to continue my life when hers was taken? What about our daughters—hers and mine? Was this the beginning of a trend?

I carried the fear and pain like a heavy cloak around my shoulders until I stooped when I walked. I went again and again to the Word of God trying to find peace. I realized that the fear and pain had become a bigger enemy than the cancer itself. I knew I must somehow continue to live life in my own way, to the very fullest, each day. This is the only possible revenge for her death.

They say time heals. Even now I wonder how long it takes for that healing to occur. I wonder how long it will be before I can pass a card counter and not cry as I look at a card that reads, "Happy Birthday to my Sister." I wonder how many years it will be before I can face June 11 without wanting to pick up the phone and wish Marilee a happy birthday. I miss her more than I can describe. Each day I pray that her faith will inspire me to move beyond the hurt and the loss.

Who shall separate us from the love of Christ? Shall tribulation, or distress, or persecution, or famine, or nakedness, or peril, or sword? . . . Yet in all these things we are more than conquerors through Him who loved us. For I am persuaded that neither death nor life, nor angels nor principalities nor powers, nor things present nor things to come, nor height nor depth, nor any other created thing, shall be able to separate us from the love of God which is in Christ Jesus our Lord.

Romans 8:35, 37–39

THE MISSING INGREDIENT

The cause of Christ can be painful and costly. It is about sacrifice. But the sacrifice is motivated by love, not fear. And the love is what sets us free. —JEANETTE THOMASON

It just couldn't get much worse than this! Caught in the very act of adultery. Dragged into the courtyard of the Temple. Publicly humiliated. Thrown in a heap at the feet of a rabbi. Within one throw of being stoned to death by an angry mob.

As with other women who briefly crossed paths with Jesus, we know nothing about her, except that she was caught in a compromising situation. Then she found herself being abused and used by the scribes and Pharisees, who were trying to trick Jesus into defying the law.

True, the Mosaic Law called for stoning to death anyone caught breaking the seventh commandment. Jesus knew it, the woman knew it, and the angry mob was bloodthirsty on the knowledge. The scribes and Pharisees were masters of every part of Scripture and watched rigidly over its interpretation, always eager to point out sins and transgressions in other people.

What an explosive situation! Jesus seated as a teacher in the courtyard. The victim crumpled in a heap on the ground. The mob, each with a stone ready to begin the punishment.

Perhaps there was a pause in the frenzy. Jesus did not respond immediately. The terrified woman was barely breathing, much less moving. The crowd began to quiet.

Jesus seized the moment to defuse the anger and hostility around Him. He did the most unexpected thing: He bent over and began to make marks in the loose dirt on the ground. Immediately the focus of the crowd changed. "What is He doing? What is He writing?" The curiosity increased. They must have looked at each other with puzzled expressions.

Slowly Jesus sat up, and with a clear but gentle voice He said, "He who is without sin among you, let him throw a stone at her first" (John 8:7). Then He went back to writing on the ground.

Much has been made of what Jesus was writing. Personally, I think that is a Pharisee-type question; it misses the point. If the content of His written message had been vital to the incident, it would have been recorded.

Visualizing the scene, it is easy to see that Jesus was changing the focus from the woman to another action. He was buying time for the anger to subside. It worked. The crowd dispersed "one by one, beginning with the oldest even to the last. And Jesus was left alone, and the woman standing in the midst" (v. 9).

What a dramatic moment in Jesus' ministry! Such simple gestures, so profound an outcome.

But the best part is yet to come. Jesus added the one missing ingredient to the equation—merciful forgiveness.

"Woman, where are those accusers of yours? Has no one condemned you?"

"No one, Lord."

"Neither do I condemn you; go and sin no more" (vv. 10–11).

Whatever our sin, Jesus is ready to lift us up, rescue us from the role of victim, and show us His love, His mercy, and His forgiveness.

Forgiveness is a complex gift. First we must be aware of our transgression. Then, in repentance, we must be open to being forgiven. (No doubt an angry mob with stones in hand could bring about a feeling of repentance rather rapidly.) But a next step might be more difficult: you must be able to forgive yourself and start down a new path. Forgiveness is a process that has a beginning, a middle, and an end. Unless the complete process comes full circle, the forgiveness is not complete, and we will find ourselves on the path back to the same sin.

The adulteress was to "go and sin no more." We assume that our sister in trouble left the gates of the Temple that day a changed woman. Her sin was more dramatically presented than most of ours, but the same love and mercy is ours for the asking.

The acceptance of forgiveness is a concept that sometimes gets overshadowed in those of us who grew up in the fire-and-brimstone era. I have even heard of support groups for folks who received a heavy dose of sin-and-shame messages. These groups encourage spiritual growth in the area of self-forgiveness and divine mercy.

Grace, forgiveness, and acceptance were always a theme of Jesus' teachings and His dealings with people. The very act of repentance is rich in forgiveness and love.

Forgiveness can change everything.

BAD NEWS

Every day we live is a precious gift of God,
loaded with possibilities to learn something new,
to gain fresh insights into His great truths.

—DALE EVANS ROGERS

Cancer came again to our peaceful shores; this time it chose my husband as host. Friends were in town from Winston-Salem to give a dinner party for our graduating Sara. A beautiful Saturday evening dinner had been planned.

But the party would be held without Mancil. Early Saturday morning he began to hemorrhage. By the time we could get to the hospital, he had lost a third of his blood supply in a matter of a few hours. "Probably something that can be fixed," his doctor said. "We'll run some tests."

Two days later came the dreaded word: *cancer.* My partner for the last thirty-five years now faced the battle of his life. Surgery removed all visible signs of the disease. But the eight-inch tumor was Stage 2 cancer, so the medical protocol stipulated chemotherapy.

Mancil was set up on a weekly schedule of chemicals. He was a real trouper, but the side effects were cruel and ugly. And after eight months, the punishment on his body took its toll with major neurological complications. The chemicals were stopped, and we set about helping him heal and returning our lives to some sort of normal routine.

Mancil was an excellent candidate for total remission. He had done extensive reading on the mind-body connection. He was a world-class positive thinker (and still is), and he was ready for a clean bill of health. He really expected remission! And remission is what he got. The doctors were delighted with the results.

To confront the terror of a life-threatening illness and then walk away is a curious feeling. We felt angry, scared, thankful, and joyous—all at the same time. It was as if we had seen the enemy, conquered him, and left. Did our lives change substantially after that? You bet. We got all our financial affairs in good order, then set about to thoroughly enjoy every minute of every blessed day.

JUST LAUGH ABOUT IT!

Nothing is too dense with misery to find something to laugh about. —MARIE CHAPIAN

How long has it been since you really had a big, jolly, belly laugh? Not a giggle. Not a polite-little-lady laugh. I mean a laugh that starts rolling up from the bottom of your feet and just bursts out—a good long bout of helpless hysterics.

Are we too busy to take time for a laugh? Are we too sophisticated to think things are funny? Are we just not joyous and slightly nuts enough to enjoy laughing?

What a pity! Laughter is healthy—both physically and emotionally. Laughing reduces tension, stimulates the immune system, releases stress, helps you sleep better, and makes you more fun to be around.

A high sense of humor also shows a high level of intelligence. And I'm convinced that somehow humor and a sense of well-being are highly connected. Laughing is like having your cake and eating it too. And it is all for free! You don't need permission. You don't need a prescription. You don't need a group. You don't need any special clothing. And there is no limit on how long you can do it. Just laugh!

Read the funnies. If you are out of the habit of laughing, it may take a minute for some of the comic strips to amuse you. Keep reading until something strikes your funny bone. Work at it. Or visit the humor section of your nearest bookstore. Many of the current funny people have put their best stories in paperback. Select one and read and laugh.

Molly Ivins's book *She Can't Say That, Can She?* hit my funny bone. I took that book to a convention with me recently. After a late-night session, I started reading the book. At first it was cute and I smiled. Then it got funny and I laughed. Within thirty minutes I was in hysterics, with tears running down my cheeks. In that hotel room, by myself, I belly laughed until the wee hours of morning. I slept like a rock, and by the next morning I felt refreshed and renewed. What a gift laughter is!

SOMEWHERE BETWEEN THE HELLOS AND GOOD-BYES

Freedom is not the right to do what we want but the power to do what we ought. —CORRIE TEN BOOM

Charlie Brown, the great philosopher, once stated, "What we need in life are more hellos and fewer good-byes." I agree. Good-byes make me sad, too, Charlie Brown.

But life is full of experiences that have hellos and good-byes built in. In fact the biggest milestones of life are usually events that have both a hello and good-bye in the same experience—graduation, birth, marriage, promotions, moving, and dying. These are the experiences that stretch our emotions, that make us face two strong, diametrical feelings at the same time.

When our oldest son married, I got in touch with this kind of emotional clash. I had never been *so* happy and *so* sad at the same time. The clash of happy and sad consumed so much emotional energy during all the festivities, I was drained dry. For days after the wedding, I just wanted to sit in the corner, suck my thumb, hold my blanket, and twirl my hair.

I was sad because I was saying good-bye to my firstborn son. We had been together for twenty-five years. I had been the main woman in his life. Well, scratch that. I had been *a* woman in his life—the one with the open billfold and the open refrigerator that continuously produced good things to eat. It was so sad to see that part of our lives go.

But I was saying hello to a new chapter, one that included the most charming, loving, precious new daughter, Melanie. She and Chase loved each other, it was obvious. They both were mature, happy, well-adjusted young adults. The wedding was a picture-book ceremony—the hope of every beautiful bride and the vicarious experience of every romantic in attendance. The future was bright and promising, and I was ecstatic. Yet how could one event be so sad and so happy at the same time?

The birth of a baby is another hello–good-bye experience. Good-bye to the freedoms of your own life, good-bye to a full night's sleep, good-bye to settling down on a rainy afternoon with a good book. But, oh my, hello to a new life! Opportunity, love, excitement, good things, and good times.

But the most important part of these hello–good-bye adventures is what's in the middle. What happens between the beginning and the end is what makes the real difference. The middle is where the meat of life is. Timing automatically gives us the hellos and the good-byes. But it is up to us to sculpt the middle in such a way that the starts and finishes are divinely justified.

A middle needs a sense of purpose big enough to include God and wide enough to include mankind. A middle needs a purpose that takes us beyond ourselves and challenges us to make life good for other people.

A middle needs to rid itself of the question, "What can I get out of this experience?" Replace it with this question: "What can I bring to this life experience that will enrich others?" A middle requires hard work and commitment. It needs imagination and courage for each day, so that when we come to the end, the good-bye, we can exit the experience with a song of thanksgiving and a sense of accomplishment.

Then as we are suspended in time, hanging between a yesterday and a tomorrow, we can make a half-turn into the next hello with anticipation and hope.

A WATER CARRIER

God loves us. It has nothing to do with whether we are attractive or lovable; He simply chooses to love us. —CYNTHIA HEALD

She was really an undesirable, especially by Jewish standards. And probably by my standards too, if I had been there. Cheap. Lowlife. Not one to associate with. Just a poor Samaritan woman now living with a man, after five failed marriages. *Pleeease!*

She arrived at the historic well, Jacob's Well, to draw water with her large clay pot. Little did she know that simple trip for water would change her life forever.

A Stranger sat at the well and asked for a drink of water. Something really fishy here! He was obviously Jewish, judging from His appearance. To start with, no man would have engaged a strange woman in conversation, period. She had had plenty of experience; she knew her place. Then, being Jewish, he would never have spoken to a Samaritan woman. She was suspicious.

And to make matters even more weird, the Stranger began talking about *living water.* What was that all about? Something about never thirsting again!

The woman listened intently. Something about this Stranger seemed so real, so honest. In spite of her lack of understanding, there was something about Him that made her want to hear more. His kind and sincere voice talked on. He suggested she go fetch her husband to come and hear the story of eternal life.

The woman hung her head in shame. Until now it had never mattered how many husbands she had had. Or who she lived with. But when the Stranger asked about her husband, it suddenly mattered a lot.

"I have no husband," she said softly.

"The fact is," the Stranger said, "you have had five husbands, and the man you now have is not your husband" (John 4:17–18 NIV).

The Samaritan woman was speechless. How could He know that? He must be a prophet or something. The air was electric. What was going on here?

The Stranger talked about worshiping the Father in spirit and truth. He said there would be no more differences in worship among national groups.

Could this possibly be the Messiah? The woman had been taught from childhood to watch for the coming Messiah. His coming would explain all things to believers.

Then the Stranger declared, "I who speak to you am he" (John 4:26 NIV).

This was big. Really big! The woman wanted to share the Stranger's message. She quickly went back to her town and gathered her friends and neighbors.

Because of the woman's testimony, many of the townspeople heard the message from the Messiah and believed! The meeting at the well was so successful and reached so many people, Jesus stayed with the Samaritans for two more days. In the end the people declared the Stranger was truly the Savior of the world.

Question: Why did Jesus select this moment and this obscure place to declare He was the Messiah? A quiet countryside in Samaria, to a simple woman living in sin. It was the first time Jesus had been willing to make this direct statement. "I am He." Why didn't Jesus go to the rabbis at the Temple? Why didn't he announce first to the faithful crowds who were following Him everywhere? Why this simple woman?

In keeping with a trend that began at His birth, Jesus' presence and mission were always announced to people from the most basic walks of life. In this case Jesus did not merely reach one woman; He reached a whole village. And not just one woman in time; He spoke to all women, virtuous or sinful, needy or well-off, bright or lacking—women of all generations to come. His far-reaching, significant messages to women showed Jesus' plan to uplift the gender, to treat women as equals in all of life. Isn't it simply amazing that two thousand years later we are still working on this lesson?

THE DAY THE BANNERS WAVED FOR SARA

Far away there in the sunshine are my highest aspirations. I may not reach them, but I can look up to see their beauty, believe in them, and try to follow where they lead. —LOUISA MAY ALCOTT

It was a day like no other. The colorful academic banners. The professors in all their regalia. Parents, proud-as-punch parents, from the four corners of the globe. Friends. Relatives. And a gentle May breeze. It was just as I had pictured it time and time again. I wanted to take in every detail so this wonderful day would never be erased from my memory.

Sara was graduating from Vanderbilt. Magna cum laude. So much of my energy had gone into helping this happen, I sometimes wondered if there would be life after today.

Even though the air was aflutter with activity, I sat quietly, remembering all that had brought us to this point. The odds were against this day ever happening. Dozens of broken bones, hospitals, traction, casts, ambulance rides, despair, pain, sleepless nights. How on earth did we get through it all and arrive at this glorious day?

Sara worked hard for this achievement. With dogged determination she set the goal and never gave up. She went to class, broken bones and all. She worked to help pay expenses. She studied hard and excelled at everything she did. Even today was no exception. She arrived at graduation with double pneumonia and a 101-degree fever. We were just thankful she wasn't in a full body cast, as she had been for her high school graduation.

We invited many of our nearest and dearest friends to join us for lunch that day, as a way of saying thank you for standing with us on this journey. The second-grade teacher who rescued Sara from a bad situation in first grade. Our dear friend who saw to it that the children and I had a ride to church each Sunday that Mancil was out of town (managing two active boys and a tiny, breakable baby was too much for one person). The friend who saw to it that Sara had a generous scholarship to attend Vanderbilt. And the precious girl who was Sara's roommate for two years at Vanderbilt. So many friends who had added a special measure of strength and encouragement along the walk.

Let's face it, this day was the result of a group effort, which is the way many of life's obstacles are overcome. We give strength and we get strength.

Glory be to God for this wonderful day! Blessed be the friends! And praise to God for His bountiful mercy and grace!

Sometimes I feel sorry for families who don't go through such trials. They really can't taste the victory.

Generally speaking, women tend to be nurturers and rescuers. When problems arise we somehow feel the need to jump right in, grab the problem, and take it as if it were our own. Then we set about trying to "fix it." By the end of any one day, we can be inundated with problems we feel responsible for. Very stressful behavior.

The next time someone (anyone—husband, child, working partner, boss, client, minister) comes to you with a problem, quickly stop and imagine yourself putting the request or problem into a beautiful, fancy shopping bag. Then set the bag down between you. You may look at the bag. You may discuss the bag and its contents. You may even move the bag around a little. But *don't pick it up!* If the contents of the bag don't belong specifically to you, don't pick it up. Leave that problem right where it belongs—at the feet of the speaker.

You may give advice about how to solve the problem. Or you may offer a suggestion of someone else who could help. But *don't pick it up!* Unless it is clearly and without question *your* problem and can *only* be solved by you, let it stay in the bag and out of your possession.

By the end of the day, you will be 50 percent freer of responsibility, and at least a dozen other people will feel great that they were able to engage in a little problem solving on their own.

It isn't easy to do. Almost without exception I will reach down and have my greedy, problem-solving fingers wrapped about those handles, ready to jerk that problem up, bag and all, and run with it. But one quick question comes to mind: "Do I own the contents of the bag?" If not, I must leave it alone.

THE WORDLESS PRAYER

In great moments life seems neither right nor wrong, but something greater, it seems inevitable.

—MARGARET SHERWOOD

The poor, sick woman was so weak, she had to approach Jesus like a shadow. She called no attention to herself. She silently positioned herself at the edge of the crowd, near the spot where Jesus was walking on the road.

A wave of hope had come over the woman. She had suffered an issue of blood for twelve years. She had exhausted every treatment available and had spent all her money—and still the blood flow continued. Not only was she growing weaker and poorer, but her condition was considered unclean. So she suffered great humiliation and isolation.

News had come to the woman of a Messiah who was traveling throughout Galilee, healing many who came to Him. Could it be? Could she possibly be healed and escape this horrible and hopeless life? Could this Man be the true Son of God?

Slowly a calm assurance covered her. This was her moment in time. She could begin to see herself healed. She visualized herself as being whole again. New strength flooded her body. A purpose, a plan, a mission formed. She would go to this Teacher and be healed. It would happen!

Being culturally unclean posed a small problem. She couldn't let the Man touch her in the healing moment. Maybe if she just reached out and unnoticeably touched His clothing, the healing could take place. Yes! That would work.

Her excitement probably carried her long past her physical reserves. Then, in the distance, she could see the crowd gathering. That must be Him. There, up ahead. Only a few more steps.

As the woman got near, she began to see more problems. People were surrounding Jesus, closing Him in. There was no way the woman could get near enough to touch His clothing. What now?

Jesus was moving, walking along the road; the crowd had to constantly shift and move along the road with Him. Maybe if she crouched down along the side of the road, she could reach out to brush a little edge of the hem of His robe.

So the woman stooped down along the side of the road. As the crowd approached, the men had to move to one side to walk around her. A perfect plan. Quickly, as the Teacher passed by, she reached out and touched Jesus' hem. A silent, very sincere prayer for healing. No words were necessary. Just a deep, abiding hope and faith in the healing process.

Then time stood still. Jesus stopped walking and He stopped talking. The crowd stopped, and everyone looked down.

"Who touched My clothes?" Jesus asked. The woman tried to become invisible. She was terrified. The plan had not worked after all. She was found out. By causing this disturbance and working her way into the crowd like that, she could be stoned to death.

But the great Teacher was looking at her with a tenderness she had never expected. Before she realized it, the entire story spilled out of her mouth. She told Jesus everything. The people looked on aghast.

Then came the words she had waited twelve years to hear: "Daughter, be of good cheer; your faith has made you well. Go in peace" (Luke 8:48). She was healed!

A force within herself, a belief, a hope, a faith so strong that not a single word had to be spoken. The woman had been capable of such great faith that it had sucked the very power from Jesus. The woman's faith had healed her!

Oh, how I love this story. It encourages my faith. The woman went twelve years without help. In fact, her condition only got worse. And yet she recognized real help when it came her way. She made a plan and put it to work. She had great timing. And once the plan was put into motion, she kept going. When the great moment came, her faith was all she needed. No words, no pleas, no more waiting. She touched and she was healed. Praise be to God.

Am I Going Crazy?

This is the kind of day that most tries my faith, my hope, and my love. There's nothing like a good crisis to increase my energy and remind me how much I need God. —ANNE CHRISTIAN BUCHANAN

The day started a little more hectic than usual. I lingered a bit at home, rushing around to get a few household chores finished.

When I walked into work, I discovered some pipes had leaked overnight. Now we not only had a big water problem but a major repair looming.

My chest started to feel a little tight, but I didn't have time to deal with the pain. A dozen phone calls. Seniors and staff needing one thing and another—all the parts I love best about my job. No time to pay attention to a few little aches and pains.

By midmorning the tightness was worse. In fact, if I really thought about it, I would have to say it was getting hard to breathe. But no time to focus on that. I had a board meeting at noon. I could drive to the meeting, then take some time to sit quietly in the car and see if I could conquer the tightness and pain. Maybe some quiet time to relax would help.

By the time I got to the building, however, I was almost breathless. The tightness and pain were escalating. *No need to panic,* I told myself. *I just need to relax and try to ignore the mounting pain.* But by now

I was sweating, my heart was pounding, and the chest pain was so bad I could hardly take a breath. I did need help! But I really didn't have time to stop. After the meeting I still had a dozen agenda items unmet for the day. A few more minutes passed.

Too bad. Meeting or no meeting, I would just have to junk the rest of the day and get help. This was obviously something serious.

I used the car phone to call the doctor. "Get to the nearest emergency room immediately," she said. "Don't drive yourself. Call someone."

The emergency room nurses had me hooked up to machines in a matter of minutes. "Lie back and relax," the nurse kept saying. Mancil was standing there looking very worried and wondering what on earth was happening.

They ran every test available. The doctor finally came in. The diagnosis: a panic attack. Not a heart attack. The muscles in my chest had gone into a hard spasm and created all the symptoms of a full-fledged heart attack. It was a type of emotional meltdown. My body was reacting to all the stress I was heaping on it.

Simple solutions: get back to the exercise routine, get more rest, slice off some of the schedule, stop some of the extra work, and give in to saying "no" more often. I was so grateful not to be going into heart surgery, it seemed like a picnic to follow the doctor's orders this time.

I don't understand how and why I continue to overextend, both physically and emotionally. But I am working hard to find a solution. That brush with what I thought was the end of me convinced me that finding a solution needs top priority. I want to finally get it right and am willing to do whatever it takes to be victorious over my own self-destruction.

TIME—FRIEND OR FOE

It is a radical faith that makes bold claims and sometimes creates tension, yet is able to stand against the tide of my world and the test of time.

—BECKY TIRABASSI

The hospital room was my home for five days while I was served powerful antibiotic drugs through a vein in my neck. The diagnosis was shingles—an exasperating, adult version of chicken pox. The endless hours and minutes dragged by like a slow, boring parade. I envisioned myself as a medical prisoner. All I could think about was how much *time* this problem was using up and how much *time* I felt I was wasting. Of course, I was so sick, I didn't have the strength to do anything but rest anyway. And since when is recuperating from an illness wasted time?

At any rate this episode shows what a time-obsessed person I am. I am a confessed time freak. I live on a tight schedule by the hour and by the minute. My days are carefully structured by what's on my calendar each morning. I keep two calendars going in order not to miss a single appointment or notes needed for the day. And when I am unable to keep the pace, I berate my failure harshly.

My husband has a curious take on time. He spends his whole life running ten to thirty minutes *ahead* of schedule. So when he says to meet him at the restaurant at 6:00, I know he means 5:45. To arrive at 6:00, as he instructed, means I am already ten to twenty minutes late!

Listen in on most any conversation and you will hear discussion on time—making time, killing time, losing track of time, time to go, time to stay, supper time, prayer time, bad times, good times. Time means different things to different people. Because *time* is neutral, it has no intrinsic value of its own. It just stands there ticking along, minding its own business. People are what gives meaning to time.

To a child sitting in a church service, time lingers too slowly. To a young couple holding hands in the park, time just races by. Sitting up all night with a sick child makes time seem endless until the dawn. A crisp, cool autumn walk can't last long enough; time is too short.

My time is a lot like my money: there's never quite enough to do all I want to do. When things really get tight, I schedule things too close together and drive myself to distraction trying to be in two places at the same time. Because of my chronic overextension, I do not see time as something friendly.

I wonder sometimes if we are being held hostage by time. There has been such an explosion of things to measure time with: calendars for every mood and every interest known to womankind. Watches that all but call your name to remind you of appointments. The whole concept of time is big business.

Does time control us? Or do we control our own time? Is time a friend? Or an enemy?

Counting time may help us know how close to lunchtime we are, but it does not tell us about the measureless possibilities contained in the next twenty-four hours.

I long for the day when I can, and will, simplify my life and begin to measure minutes and days by the good times of life, the rich experiences and relationships I share with special people every day. I want to measure time, not by watches and desk calendars, but by the life and love with which I fill my days. I think this method of counting minutes will have something to do with the way we measure time in eternity—by quality, not quantity.

In the Palm of His Hand

Go out into the darkness and put your hand into the hand of God. That shall be to you better than light and safer than a known way.

—MINNIE LOUISE HASKINS

It was a routine physical. The doctor was out on an emergency so I saw the nurse practitioner. She never gave a hint that anything could be wrong. Later I saw that she had written something on the mammogram request that instructed the radiologist to look carefully at a certain area.

Schedule an appointment for the mammogram. See you next year.

A week later I'm at Baptist Hospital for the mammogram. Wait for the film to be developed. Small problem. A smudge or something on the film. Second try. I complied without the least hint of anxiety. I might have been a tad agitated at the extra time it took, but I wasn't worried. It wouldn't be much longer.

The nurse came out. A questionable area—just a slight thickening of breast tissue. Probably nothing to worry about at all. But, just to be safe, let's do an ultrasound. Further delay. Didn't they realize I was a busy woman—places to go, people to see, meetings to attend?

I waited in the darkened examining room, equipment humming all around me. I felt not a single tinge of fear or anxiety. Breast cancer would never happen to me. I practiced all kinds of good health measures—always had checkups right on schedule. I did self-exams, just as I had been taught.

The doctor slowly moved the ultrasound instrument over my breast while she watched the monitor. "Has anyone in your family had breast cancer?"

Not a good question! I did not want to go into this discussion right now. Somehow even the question seemed to make me more vulnerable. I didn't want her to know that the hideous disease had taken my precious sister only a short two years earlier. I didn't want to even think about it, much less connect that sadness to this moment.

But the doctor made the connection very quickly and very emphatically.

Next stop, surgeon's office. Now the fear level began to rise a little. But the greatest worry was my family. They just couldn't find out about this. Marilee's death was still too fresh in our lives—too scary, too raw. My mother was still in a lot of grief. We were still reeling from the shock that *our* family could be struck by this dastardly thief.

In addition, Mancil had just finished an eight-month course of chemotherapy following his surgery for cancer. The side effects had been horrendous. He was tired and weak—not able to take on a new crisis of this magnitude. My sons were just now able to face their father's illness. And Sara needed me healthy every day. No one would be able to sustain a new blow like this.

I carefully explained the circumstances to each doctor, each receptionist, and each nurse. I asked them to write in big red letters on my chart, *"Do not call home phone with test results."* It was just a precautionary measure. No need to get everyone upset at this point. Anyway, this couldn't be cancer. It didn't feel like cancer!

The fine-needle aspiration went well. Not pleasant, but not a big deal. I left the office and honestly put the whole thing behind me. Things were hectic at work and I had a million things on my mind. Even though I faced the weekend with no test results, I simply did not give it a second thought.

On Tuesday I was sitting at my desk, trying to finish a report on a short deadline. The phone rang.

"Dr. Hamilton speaking. I have the results of your biopsy. I found cancer cells."

Blank. Silence. Disbelief. Wrong number maybe.

Somewhere I found a voice, and with more confidence than I felt, I said, "Schedule surgery as soon as possible."

Now the doctor was surprised. "Don't you want to come into the office and discuss your options?"

"We just did discuss it," I said. "You said, 'Cancer.' I said, 'Cut it out!' End of discussion."

I closed the door of my office and sat in the stillness for a while. I don't know how long. This was beyond tears. I just sat.

I prayed. "This isn't fair. You know that, Lord. My sister died of cancer. My husband had cancer. Now I have cancer. You know that is just not fair." The rest of my prayer had no words; I trusted the Holy Spirit to fill in the blanks for me. Slowly a quiet strength began to form down deep in my being. I could do this. I *had* to do this! I wasn't sure how, but I would get through it—one hour at a time—by leaning on the Everlasting Arms.

After a while I started to pick up one piece at a time and fit them all together. First, I simply could not fall apart. My family would be looking to me and would react based on how I was reacting. Facing things honestly and head-on would be the best plan.

I called the family together that night to give them the news. They were stunned. Cold terror on inside and trying to be brave on the outside. The faith and presence of each person gave strength and courage to the others. My mother was strong, as always, in the time of crisis. What a tower of strength. How does she do it? Mancil pulled the remnants of his strength together. The children were upset, but so supportive. Together we stood firm for each other. Oh, the richness of a family together!

Two days later Mancil and I left home for the hospital early in the morning. I don't know where we found the courage to make that drive. What I didn't know was that my dear working companions at the office were meeting in Fran's office, and were, at that very moment, holding hands in prayer for me.

I stand here now to testify that right then a peace that went beyond understanding passed over and through my being, bringing a calmness. There could only be one explanation: they called on the peace and power of the Holy Spirit to flood my soul like a river. I simply released my fear into His strength and rolled off to surgery.

I was home within twenty-four hours. When the doctor called to give us the lab report, he said, "I have the best news I could possibly give to a cancer patient. I got it all. No more cancer. No chemotherapy. You are going to be fine."

I don't know why I got a good report and Marilee did not. I don't know why I am still OK and Marilee is gone. My family and friends prayed, and her family and friends prayed. If we had prayed longer or more fervently, would God have saved Marilee? Did I contribute less than enough to her healing?

Only God knows when a disease is irreversible. All I know is that Marilee had a cancer very different from mine, a cancer that killed. I must believe that God alone knows the plan and that, because we are mortal, some diseases kill and others do not. As I release my prayers to the God of the universe, I must leave life-and-death decisions in His hands. I must trust this divine decision and look for the health that is deeper than death.

I hope I can learn to do that.

UP A TREE AND OUT ON A LIMB

Whatever God asks you to be, He enables you to be! —ANNE ORTLAND

The gospel writers were generous to recount many of Jesus' personal encounters with people along the way. As I think about so many New Testament encounters, it seems almost every one occurred while Jesus was on His way to another engagement—on the road, as He passed by, while He was teaching, by the side of the pool.

Jesus was a busy man. He had a lot to accomplish in only three short years, so there was not a minute to waste. No matter where Jesus encountered a need, He stopped to deal with the person on the spot.

Like the day He was on His way through Jericho and He came upon Zacchaeus, who was up a tree and out on a limb, in more ways than one. Zacchaeus was a tax collector. This was a job people took if they absolutely couldn't find any other way to earn a living. Being a tax collector branded you a traitor and estranged you from rest of the citizens. The community despised tax collectors (I suppose not unlike today).

In New Testament times, these collectors were allowed to gouge as much money as possible from the citizens. The amounts were never checked on, and the collector made his money by overtaxing and keeping large sums of income for himself. It was all legal, but not exactly a way of winning popularity contests. If the collector did his job well, he could become a wealthy member of the community; but money would have to take the place of friends. As a despised tax collector, Zacchaeus did not appear on anyone's guest list.

No wonder he was on the periphery of the excitement when Jesus came along. A rather undignified figure, sitting out on a tree limb, trying to see what the fuss was all about.

And wouldn't you know that is exactly where Jesus stopped. Then He announced He was having lunch with Zacchaeus. Every blue blood in town was miffed that Jesus would stoop to eat with scum of the city. What was Jesus thinking?

But, knowing Jesus, can you think of any other possibility? Jesus knew Zacchaeus needed a life-changing experience. He knew Zacchaeus hungered for acceptance, for meaning in his dismal life, and for a center of peace in his soul. By now, Zacchaeus's defenses were down; he had no pride to overcome. His self-sufficiency could no longer sustain him. He needed Jesus.

I believe that being up a tree and out on a limb is the *perfect* place to come face-to-face with Jesus. That particular position puts us in a receptive frame of mind. Remember how fast Zacchaeus got down out of that tree? And in no time at all, they were all eating lunch at the Zacchaeus house. (I hope Mrs. Zac was good with unexpected company.)

When Jesus finds us in the spot of our greatest need, when He sees us most defenseless, most vulnerable, most needy, that's when His strength is made perfect. That's when He can fill in our gaps to make us whole. That's when the Everlasting Arms reach out and say, "Come on down. Let's go to your place and talk."

God offers us so much in Christ—a life with eternal possibilities. But we have to get off the limb and out of that tree.

LISTEN!

One thing that God has taught me is that movement needs to be in a forward direction. . . . Going forward is the response of God's people when they have taken the time to hear him.

—DR. SUZAN D. JOHNSON COOK

Sh-h-h-h. Don't say anything! Just listen. What do you hear? People talking? Household machines churning away? Phones ringing? What?

A curious thing, listening. We have so perfected the art of selective listening that we can encounter a dozen sounds at one time but only hear one of them. Somehow we have trained our brains to accept only a small portion of the many sounds that come in through our ears. That skill of selective listening can work for our good, but it can also be a problem.

For example, what happens when you say, "Someone needs to carry the garbage out"? Chances are, no one moves, because every person within earshot used selective listening. So your statement just sailed through thin air.

On a hectic day, or in a large group situation, or in a room full of children, selective listening is an essential means to survival. But the trouble comes when we put selective listening on automatic pilot. Let me give you another familiar example. You're having a one-on-one conversation, and you realize the voice inflection of the other person has just indicated a question mark. But you weren't listening to the words, so you have no clue whatsoever how to respond. You weren't really listening. Have you been there? Scary, isn't it?

I perfected the art of selective listening when the children were young. Mancil and I spawned three really big talkers. They started early and spoke lots and long. Our ears went into overload by noon most days, but the conversations went on. Jason, especially, could tell when I went into my "general response" mode, nodding and saying "uh huh" occasionally, whether it was a fitting response on not. He would often take my face between his fat little hands, pull me down to his level, and say very earnestly, "*Wisten* to me!" And then I really *wistened*.

It is time to reinvent real listening, to establish contact all over again. We need to listen to others, really hear the sounds and words that describe their hurts, their successes, their hopes. We need to hear the words, so we can laugh with others, cry with others, and encourage others. We need to listen with our hearts as well as ears, so that we not only hear their words, but we hear the part of the message they can't put into words. We need to really hear the fear, the longing, and the distress. Only when we have the total message can we respond appropriately. To be Christian is to learn to listen to people as Jesus did and to care about what we hear.

But perhaps the most significant listening skill we can cultivate is listening to God. When we are in communication with God, our prayers are usually so full of asking and giving directions that we talk right past the listening part. I sometimes picture God taking my face in his hands and saying, "Listen to me!"

The biblical account of Mary and Martha serves us well here. Martha complained that Mary was not busy with the household responsibilities. But Jesus told Martha, "You are worried and upset about many things, but only one thing is needed. Mary has chosen what is better, and it will not be taken away from her" (Luke 10:41–42 NIV). Mary was simply listening. Being with Jesus. Concentrating. Sharing the presence of God.

To listen is to hear God's truth, to hear answers that summon us to greater commitment. We need spaces of silent attention toward God. Divine conversation. Are you listening?

STRESS BUSTER

Smile. **It beats me how this works, but it works for me every single time. When I am stressed, my face ties itself up into hard, muscular knots. My eyebrows knit together, my teeth are clamped shut, and my neck is almost paralyzed with tension. When I stop and smile, however, it just turns things around.**

Lift your eyebrows, relax your neck, and smile a big sincere smile. Not only does this reduce your stress, but it can slowly change your attitude about what's causing your stress. And if you keep that smile in place long

enough, it makes everyone else wonder what you've been up to.

So, put on a happy face!

The End of the Rope

Without the burden of afflictions it is impossible to reach the height of grace. The gifts of grace increase as the struggles increase. —ST. ROSE OF LIMA

You've heard the saying, "When you get to the end of your rope, tie a knot and hang on."

I reached the end of my rope one day about six months after my surgery for breast cancer. It was also shortly after a traumatic job change, after an accident with Sara (I fell carrying her and broke her legs and one arm), after I lost my sister, and after my husband's cancer surgery and chemotherapy, all within a relatively short period of time.

Is it any wonder that the final straw came in the form of a severe case of shingles? I endured a week in the hospital, which was a feat in itself. Once I got out of that quarantined room, I made a run for it. I quickly went out to lunch and then back to work.

Within two days I was sitting at my desk, holding the end of my rope. And I'm pretty sure there was not enough rope left to tie a knot in. I had to have help just to make it to a car to be driven home.

My strength, physically, mentally, and spiritually, was totally gone. I had come to the end of being able to cope with a single thing. All I could do was go straight to my room and straight to bed. I had to literally crawl on my hands and knees up the stairs; I couldn't even stand unassisted.

What gets us in that kind of a situation? How do we get to the end of our rope in such dire situations? My hunch is that this is not a unique occurrence. I can picture you now as you read this. Are you nodding your head and saying, "Yes, I've been there"?

Let's see what we can learn about preventing rope burn. No one will argue the point that bad things *do* happen, and sometimes they happen in rapid succession. So how do we keep from being plowed under by the burden?

I will admit to being at some fault. I often don't allow myself nearly as much healing time as I would insist on for my family members, or my staff, or even my friends. I wisely advise others, "Take a few days. Let your spirit come back to life."

Then why is it so hard for *me* to apply that advice to *my* life? Somehow I must still be operating in the Superwoman mode, although I thought I gave that up years ago. I see the family looking worried and sad . . . and hungry. So I just get up! Once a mom lifts her head off the pillow, the word spreads quickly: "She's up! She's well!" And the pace picks back up to full throttle.

Somehow we need to establish a schedule that allows Moms of Households to have real recovery time.

In addition, we need an intensity clause. Have you seen the T-shirt declaring, "When Mom ain't happy, ain't nobody happy"? It's true. When I'm sad or grieving, everyone else in the family mirrors the feeling. I get so depressed seeing the long, sad faces that I opt for a happy face as soon as possible. We need a clause in our household working agreement specifying that, when the situation warrants, we can be as sad as we need to be, for as long as we need to be, without bringing the whole house down. Our sadness or sickness needs to be respected, not mirrored.

Finally, we need an agreement with ourselves that we can be honest with our own feelings and needs. It's OK to say, "I am feeling really sad (or bad, or sick, or painful) right now. I will be better later. But for now, I need to go to my room and be alone. I'll let you know when I'm better."

And then, we need to be very aware of the big difference between "better" and "well."

I lift up my eyes to the hills—
where does my help come from?
My help comes from the LORD,
the Maker of heaven and earth.
Psalm 121:1–2 NIV

THE HAPPIEST THINGS IN LIFE ARE FREE

Don't cry over things that were or things that aren't. Enjoy what you have now to the fullest.

—BARBARA BUSH

It's a funny discussion, when you think about it—discussing what makes people happy. Can you imagine people of two or three generations back having a discussion on happiness? Then people just did what they had to do to survive, and probably never had a thought about what brought them pleasure. They just lived.

But today the search for happiness consumes our time, our thoughts, our money, our buying power, and usually our dreams. How can we find happiness? What makes some people happy while others drown in their own sadness?

One thing is certain: money, fame, beauty, marriage and education are *not* ingredients of happiness. Even though many people spend lifetimes pursuing any one of these goals, we know lasting pleasure seldom comes in these packages. Of course I wouldn't be one to turn down any one of these conditions, but I have been around the block enough times to know they are not the end of the happiness search.

So one day I set about finding where happiness comes from. I interviewed happy people and sad people. I interviewed contented people and zestful people. Four facts quickly emerged as the recurring theme in happiness, with one being the universal first answer.

1. **Invest in the happiness of other people.** No one mentioned their latest cruise, or their success in the stock market, or building bigger barns as their road to happiness.

   One eighty year old told of how she enjoys playing the piano and organ for others to enjoy. She goes to shelters, retirement homes, and classrooms to play music for people to sing to, listen to, and enjoy. She says that walking into the different facilities and encountering gloom and hopelessness gives her such a charge, because she knows that within a few minutes she will turn the atmosphere completely around. It is a rare person who can sit through one of her singalongs without joining in. At the end of an hour, she leaves happy, smiling faces.

   Turn your attention to people around you. What can you do to make the world a better place? Can you spread some happiness? Do you have a hobby or could you cultivate an interest (gardening, birds, poetry, collecting, photography) that can be shared with others? Spreading cheer to other people is the central ingredient of truly happy people. People who have regular schedules of volunteerism report a sensation like "runner's high," followed by a feeling of great satisfaction. I would call that happiness.
2. **Enjoy the simple pleasures of life.** Find the small things that give you a big high. Big accomplishments, stupendous vacation trips,

and winning the lottery are all fun and can produce happiness. But temporary, euphoric highs fade. For lasting happiness, you have to recognize the good things in daily life. You know the old saying: Take time to smell the flowers.

I have a friend who is mother to four young children, one of them with a disability. Her days are a tangled mess of dirty clothes, nonstop activity, half-eaten jelly sandwiches, and noise. But Connie is one of the happiest people I know. "I just go with the flow," she says. "And every day is a new adventure." She loves to cook and delights in an opportunity to bake a fancy cake for special occasions. Sometimes I look at her and think that if she can be that happy in her situation, anyone can be happy.

3. **Don't look for happiness.** If there is only one aspect of this discussion that sticks with you, let it be this: you will never find happiness when you're looking for it. *Happiness is what happens on the road to doing something else.* Being a happy person is not a goal, it is a part of the journey. Focus on others, expand an interest, take a class, learn something new, volunteer for a church job—anything! Just get busy with life and happiness will find you.
4. **Act happy.** One of my favorite songs is from the musical *The King and I*—"Whenever I Feel Afraid." I have memorized every word of that song, and I sing it when I feel a little scared. But one of the phrases fits here as

well: "'Cause when you fool the people you fear, you fool yourself as well."

If you act happy, look happy and sound happy, you can actually fool yourself into being happy. Going through the motions of acting happy can actually trigger happy emotions. After a while, being happy will feel just as comfortable as nursing your unhappiness. Happiness is a habit.

The Gifts of Christmas

Make a memory with your children,
Spend some time to show you care;
Toy and trinkets can't replace those
Precious moments that you share. —ELAINE HARDT

Of all the Christian events we celebrate, we put the greatest emphasis on Christmas. We celebrate and celebrate and celebrate. Our grandmothers would be quick to remind us that years ago we did not get involved in preparing for Christmas until after Thanksgiving. But now store decorations go up by Halloween, and in some cases the Christmas items for sale stay out all year. Christmas is big business.

And I, for one, am one of the major culprits. I love Christmas and start buying gifts by June or July. By August I have all the decorations planned for multiple trees and even have an entertainment schedule in mind. By Christmas Eve I am so tired, I sometimes nod off during the church service. But I can put on one good Christmas celebration.

Ever in the uppermost part of my concentration, however, is the reason for the season. I love the festivities, but I am focused on the Gift, because I take time regularly to stop and appreciate every part of the preparation.

I would like to give four gifts for you to use at Christmastime to keep you and your family focused on the real meaning of the celebration.

First, I want to give you a *gift of time.* This gift would include a time of daily discussion about the true meaning of Christmas. It would also contain a time of spiritual renewal, a time of family strengthening though a shared project, and a time to share more of yourself with your children.

The gift of time challenges you to prepare for Christmas in advance so that the days just before Christmas can be spent in the spirit of loving and sharing. Make the things you do count for double. Don't just spend your time preparing for the holiday. Invite your children to share in the preparation so that a happy process is the result rather than just a product. Use an advent calendar or an advent wreath to keep the family focused.

Second, I would like to give you a *gift of awareness.* Often we get so caught up in a whirlwind of activities that the entire process dulls our senses and numbs our awareness. Perhaps the numerous decisions about gifts and the constant outpouring of money are so painful that we prefer not to dwell on what we're doing. But our little children quickly pick up this attitude of rush and greed. Santa Claus and commercialism do not cause children to miss the point of Christmas. That happens when we as Christian parents fail to set the proper example.

Set aside a few minutes each day to reflect on what took place that first Christmas. Become aware of what your days mean to you. Think about your feelings, your spiritual experiences, and your relationships. Concentrate on what your activities teach your children. Remember, you are passing feelings and attitudes on to your children. You are setting an example, spiritual or otherwise, about how Christmas should be celebrated.

Third, I want to give you a *gift of tradition*. The single factor that sets a holiday apart from an ordinary day is tradition. A holiday is something that recurs year after year. Hundreds of years ago people celebrated Christmas. And for centuries to come people will continue to celebrate this holy day.

In our mobile and changing society, traditions are a strengthening base. Traditions help children become aware that things have a past, a present, and a future. Traditions help them to see themselves as a part of history, a part of a whole.

Develop holiday traditions in your family. Plan several meaningful activities or rituals and continue these each year.

Most families have the tradition of Santa Claus. This Christmas game is one of the oldest and most widely used holiday traditions. When Santa Claus is a part of the total celebration of the Christmas season, your family can identify with Christmas festivities around the world.

Finally, I want to give you a *gift of togetherness*. Included in this gift would be the hope that any conflict in your family would be resolved by reflecting on the message of love that the Christ child brought.

Play the following game, which will enhance feelings of acceptance and love within your family. Go to each person in the family each day and say, "You are special to me during this holiday season because . . ."

Spread your feelings of togetherness beyond the family circle. While your family may want to make a special effort to do something for families who have special needs, don't overlook neighbors and friends. Friends who live near you and those at church also need the warmth of your family's love.

Now, give yourself a fifth gift: the *gift of joy*. Make it your own special gift as you interact with your children and friends. Make it a time of spiritual renewal. During this holiday season grow toward a new dimension of holiday celebration. Make it a Christmas to share *more*, not less, with your children. Then you will have gained a new appreciation of the joy of giving. And you will have received the greatest gift of all as you experience God's love.

What Makes Life Good?

When you have clung to Jesus through pain and problems and experienced His amazing grace, you find joy in Him. —JOANN LEVEL

As I bounce through the Autumn of my life, it has become vitally important to me to discover the real importance of life. Frankly, up until now I haven't had time to think about it; I was too busy living. But now I'm curious. What has made my life such a satisfying venture? Why do I usually have a pleasant feeling of contentment and deep-rooted meaning to my days?

I've been taking a long look at what I feel are positive characteristics as well as places where I've missed the point. So, for what it's worth, this is what's important to me.

This may or may not be what is important to you, but perhaps it will lead you to your own search for meaning.

For me, being able to use my God-given ability to make choices and control my own destiny remains a top priority. Within God's purpose and plan for my life, I have been given a free will to make choices and to become the best person I can be. It is up to me, in right relationship to God, to decide what path my life should take.

When we are enjoying an illusion of control over our own destinies, we tend to feel empowered with a greater ability to cope with the traumas of life. You have read enough about my life by this point to know that it has been no piece of cake. I have faced plenty of challenges that tested the fabric of my being. Most of the challenges were beyond my control, or they never would have happened. But within each trauma were options. Sometimes the choices were narrow, without much wiggle room. But there were usually some points that I could have a measure of control over.

At times I took control and made choices when it didn't seem that options were available. When Sara was five, for example, she had a bad accident while playing at a friend's house. She broke both legs and an arm. After three months of never-ending disaster, the doctors decided the next step in her recovery would be major surgery on both legs to insert metal rods in her bones. The surgery and recovery would take many months and would have to be repeated every few years as she grew. We sat in overwhelming devastation at the news. We were already tired beyond reason. Facing at least another year of extended hospitalization, with an uncertain outcome, seemed so horrible. Our family life was suffering. Our health was breaking under the strain. The doctor continued, racing along with explanations, dates, and schedules.

Suddenly a burst of energy surged through me and I said, "No!" The room was full of orthopedic interns and residents, in addition to the specialists. A hush fell over the room like a pall. The students' eyes got as big as saucers, and everyone was looking at me. What a spot to be in. But somehow I continued and grew stronger with every word. "We won't be doing that. We have experienced all the suffering we can handle at this time. There won't be any surgery."

I can't begin to describe the look on those doctors' faces. Even my husband was looking at me with a mixed look of surprise and relief. I just took back some control over our lives and made a decision I thought was best for us.

That wasn't the last discussion I had with the specialists over that issue. But when the dust settled and Sara's recovery progressed, I saw that it had been the right decision. I praise God for that. But the empowerment of taking control of that situation pulled me back on a road to recovery for myself.

Retaining control of your own life can be especially difficult for women. We have been culturized into certain roles. "Good" wives and mothers know their places and generally do as they are told; big decisions are left to the men to make. Women traditionally have had little control over their own destinies. Thank God, this is changing, and the young women of today are making choices for themselves.

Staying in control is a huge factor for older adults. As we age, we begin to lose little parcels of control, then larger parcels of control. So much of the despair and depression among the elderly is due to a loss of control over when they eat, what they eat, what they wear, where they can go, how they can get there, etc. It has been shown time and again that a frail, elderly person will become more alert, active, and happy when he or she experiences small opportunities to make choices and exercise some measure of control.

Teaching children this element of self-control is so important. Begin early by allowing children to have some options. What do you want for lunch? What do you want the family to do tonight? Which shirt do you want to wear? What shoes go with that? If appearance is very important to you, then you may have to give choices within a certain range. But how exciting it is to see my five-year-old friend Skye at the shopping mall wearing her Snow White dress with her frog rain boots on the wrong feet. You talk about cutting her own deals—Skye has been allowed to make her own choices from a very early age. She will grow up to be an empowered decision maker, controlling the flow of her own happiness.

Having no control over your life diminishes your self-esteem and compromises your sense of satisfaction. As I look to the Winter of my life, I pray that I can continue to be my own person, making bountiful decisions within the boundaries of God's love and purpose.

And I do hope I can find some green frog rain boots in my size.

BAH, HUMBUG!

A wise woman can tell the difference between what is make believe and the here and now.

—BARBARA JENKINS

By anyone's standards I am a Christmas nut. I plan for Christmas all year. By October I'm hitting high gear on the holiday express—cooking, freezing, shopping, and planning decorations. So I don't take kindly to the Bah Humbugs of the world raining on my Christmas parade.

If by some chance you, dear reader, could possibly fall into that category, let's talk about it. Let me see if I can get you to trade your moans and groans for season's greetings.

Humbugs say, "Christmas is just too commercialized, I hate to participate because it's nothing but a big spending spree."

Christmas Nuts say, "Christmas is no more commercialized than you let it be. When you make provisions for gifts all through the year, it lessens the pressure in December. Shop sales and flea markets during the summer."

Humbugs say, "I hate to spend money on gifts that people don't even appreciate. We all have too much stuff anyway!"

Christmas Nuts say, "Give thoughtful gifts, not expensive gifts. Make gifts, bake gifts. Give gifts of time, or poetry, or personally written stories. Give tulip bulbs or crocus bulbs or tea bag packages or sea shells. People will learn to anticipate your gifts because they are so thoughtful and not commercial."

Humbugs say, "She never sent me a thank-you note for last year's gift, so I'm not giving her anything this year."

Christmas Nuts say, "Hey, what's the big deal? Give because you love to give—no other reason. Gifts are an extension of your good will. They show folks that you are thinking about them at this special season. Enjoy!"

Humbugs say, "People spend too much for decorations. They miss the point of Christmas."

Christmas Nuts say, "Celebrate, sing, meet, greet each other, and have the biggest, happiest party you can have. It's Christmas, the birthday of the Christ child. What could be more deserving of a celebration?"

Humbugs say, "Christmas is just so depressing. It reminds me of the bad times when I was a child."

Christmas Nuts say, "Create some new memories for yourself! Find a family or a child who has no prospects for a good Christmas. Get involved with that family. As you create good memories for others, you will be giving yourself new, beautiful memories."

Humbugs say, "Christmas is just such a letdown afterward. I'm depressed all through January."

Christmas Nuts say, "Be more realistic in your expectations of Christmas and carry over some of the outreach projects you do during the holidays. There are people in need of care and attention even in January. Extend the celebration time by planning for more contacts and ministry efforts in the new year."

There is no room for Humbugs! Christmas does not have to be miserable unless we want it to be. God came down on that holy night to show us love. Join in the joy!

THE RELUCTANT ADULT

Goals are access lines to the future. They allow us to run the race with the finish line firmly established. —EMILIE BARNES

Chase, our oldest, is a classic example of first-child personality. We call him our "Do-Right Daddy." Which is not to say he hasn't done his fair share of testing limits. But by and large Chase naturally chooses "right." He feels more comfortable with lots of rules to define his boundaries.

So it was no wonder when, during his early teen years, he began questioning the future. It began to look a little scary to become all grown up and not have parental guidelines. He sat one day, apparently contemplating this possibility, when he sighed real big and said, "Is there anything I can be when I grow up—besides an adult?"

It is hard to let go of the familiar and face a changing future. Most of us prefer things to occur in expected patterns with predictable outcomes. We are content with the same well-worn routine that is recognizable. Like Chase, we think it would be comfortable if life could always stay the same, with the stability and security we crave. Granted, life wouldn't be very exciting. But it would certainly be safe and secure.

Growing up is a bittersweet experience in which we learn again and again that we must let go of being a child in order to move forward. We must relinquish certain pleasures in order to discover greater ones.

But now I find myself in the same place Chase was, with a certain fear and apprehension of the future. I want to sit down with him and say, "Hey, Chase, as I age is there anything else I can be besides *old*?"

I am just now getting used to the routine of being a mature, middle-aged adult. And frankly, I'm a little afraid of what comes next. True, I've seen a lot of folks do an exceptional job of aging. They continue learning, they continue to invest in the lives of others, they stay fit and healthy.

But we all know it doesn't always happen like that. I also have encountered beautiful people who grew sour and sad. They became introverted and let their worlds shrink into tiny, self-centered planets with only themselves as friends. What if that happens to me?

Sometimes I think Chase was right to question the need to move on. I'd like to stay right here. Unfortunately, it just doesn't work that way. Life is always moving us forward, giving us new challenges as well as new opportunities. Time passes, changes come, and we must change with them. The God we worship makes all things new and is never finished with us.

After much thought and a couple of college degrees later, Chase did solve his dilemma. He found out how to take the best of his childhood along with him into adult life. Chase is a recreational therapist, so he plays for a career. Great plan. He also helps others get in touch with play and recreational experiences.

My world cannot stand still. But I can become who I want to be in later life. And I don't have to be old if I don't want to. Faith and understanding will lead me into wider horizons.

Give and Take

Don't go to your grave without flying a kite, skipping rope, going barefoot, catching fireflies, and jumping in a mud puddle. Let go and live.

—BARBARA JENKINS

My precious friend Margaret is battling for her very life. The cancer continues to grow despite all the chemo and radiation. As the cancer grows, so does her pain. Her frail body is bent with the burden. It is a sad thing to see, until you get to her face. Even in pain, Margaret's face is clear and bright and happy. Her body tells the physical story; her face tells the spiritual story.

I talked to Margaret today. I asked her how she was feeling. In a soft little voice, she gave this account: "Well, I would have to say it has been a rough week. The doctors are not pleased with my progress. But one good thing happened. I was able to help someone. You know, Elsie broke her hip. I've been too sick to go see her, but I talked to her on the phone today. She was able to tell me how badly she hurt. She knew I would understand her pain. So she felt better when she was able to tell me all about it. And I felt a lot better because I was able to help her."

Did you read that right? Margaret felt better because she could reach out—she could give something to another person. Even in her own pain and discomfort, Margaret was trying to find ways of reaching out to others.

Giving is like that. I have never met a giving person who was miserable. Takers, on the other hand, are miserable. But givers find a reason to live, no matter their present circumstances. And the totally unexplainable thing is that the more you give, the more you get in return. Takers never quite get that point.

Service to others is a privilege and a joy. Giving to others fully and unselfishly is what makes your cup run over. Taking and whining empty your cup dry. Only concern for other people fills cups. Margaret saw the pain in another, and knowing the solace for that pain, she set about to ease the hurting. Giving multiplied to make them both feel better.

Sometimes giving is just listening, sometimes it is delivering a meal, or it's a hug, or a happy word of encouragement, or maybe just a smile.

Give to uplift, to support, to encourage. Never give to a person's dependence. If your reaching out will, in any way, help a person continue in a path of depending on handouts or a path of continuing in need, plan another approach. Give to support independence.

Then be ready to enjoy your own feeling of well-being. Givers feel *good*. The more encumbered you are with cares and discouragement, the more you need to give.

WHINE, WHINE, WHINE

Life is what we make it, always has been, always will be. —GRANDMA MOSES

The day I discovered the secret about whiners, I felt like the luckiest person alive. Understanding whiners freed me from hour upon hour of listening to people with long lists of chronic complaints.

You know what that secret is? Whiners and complainers just love their problems and are willing to defend those problems to the bitter end! That's right. They want to hold on to that misery. And the absolute last thing they want is for you to offer a solution or to help them out of their situations.

The number one thing whiners need and want is an audience. Once they find a listening ear, they can rail on for hours about child-rearing problems, marriage difficulties, job troubles, or in-law conflicts. They are free to corner you eyeball to eyeball or catch you on the phone. Either way, you're in for it, with the whiner utterly impervious to any input you have.

And if by some miracle a whiner's problem does accidentally meet up with a solution, never worry. Within a few days, she will have managed to come up with a completely new misery.

What to do?

First, turn on a mental tape recorder just to double-check your own conversation. Are you a whiner? If so, remedy that situation immediately. It is whining when you constantly discuss your problems ad nauseam, without even a brief thought of working toward a reasonable solution.

This is not the same as discussing, for a short duration, some specific need, with the hope that your listening friend might shed some light on the immediate dilemma or help you explore alternatives.

Whining friends certainly come under the heading of difficult people. When difficult friends continue to pull you down and abuse your friendship, you need to help them see that your relationship can be much more meaningful to you both if you can talk in a more adult pattern. Whiners may not be aware of how much pain and discomfort they inflict on others.

What should you say to a whiner? Something like, "You know, you have a real problem there. But I don't know how to help you. Was there something specifically you had in mind for me to do?" (Be sure not to take the problem away from said friend. It's her problem. Leave it in her possession.)

That should cut the whining down to a manageable size. Or simply ask the question, "I see your difficulty. What do you plan to do about it?" Just asking this question may send up a flare, indicating that when you discuss life's dilemmas, you expect to get around to the solution sooner rather than later.

BIG MAMA'S CORNBREAD

Whether or not we pay attention to it, all of life is a lesson. Every moment allows an assessment of the world around us and the one within us.

—BARBARA ROBERTS PINE

The very best treasures we have in life are the ones we don't even realize until it is too late, until the whole good thing has just slipped right through our fingers. I'm talking about the rich family stories that every extended family has.

As life marches on, we look back and realize what a big mistake it was not to write down more of the very important stories as we went along. Or we could have recorded those important stories on tape or film. But by the time you think about it, the family history nuggets are dim and mostly forgotten. I am in the process now of begging my older cousins to help fill in my blank spaces by telling the old stories from my family.

My grandparents, Big Mama and Big Daddy Dale, both lived into their late nineties. They had never heard of cholesterol, diet supplements, aerobic exercise, triglycerides, or CAT scans. They didn't worry a whit about how to live. They just lived—and they lived each day to the fullest.

At age forty-something, Big Dad had a heart attack and was forced to retire from the pastorate in Tahoka, Texas. The doctor at that time predicted Big Dad wouldn't have a very long life, so he should take it easy and make his days last as long as possible. Big

Dad, of course, outlived every doctor he ever had and preached the funeral services for most of them. And he preached most every Sunday in whatever pulpit needed a preacher. He kept his own yard and garden, mowing and trimming by hand—no power equipment—until he was eighty-five.

On a regular basis we went to Big Mama's house for lunch. Fried chicken, fried squash, fried okra, black-eyed peas, and green beans cooked in bacon drippings. And the cornbread! She insisted what gave her cornbread its extraordinary taste was the little metal bowl she mixed it in and the broken wooden spoon she stirred with. Whatever the secret was, no one has ever made cornbread exactly like that. We would eat until we had to have help getting up from the table.

Big Mama ate all her meals as she cooked and as she cleaned the dishes after the meal. She never sat at the table with the family. And she cleaned every plate by eating "all the best parts" we left behind.

George and Frances Jane Dale were a West Texas institution. Big Dad led more revivals, conducted more weddings, and preached more funerals than any ten preachers added together. When they retired, Big Dad and Big Mama "held court" in their tiny, white frame house on 25th Street. People came from all over West Texas to ask advice, get counseling, get married, or discuss church problems. They always had time to give a word from the Lord to every pilgrim who passed their way. They loved people and loved all their legion of friends.

On their seventy-fifth wedding anniversary, the White House called with congratulations. Of course, their house was full of well-wishers at the time. Big Mama answered the phone and when the operator said, "This is the White House calling," she answered without hesitating, "Well, could you call back later? I have all my friends here right now."

Friends were always top priority.

AFTERWORD

Today the last thousand words of this book were put on paper. The computer screen will soon go dark, and *Living Simply in God's Abundance* will be history. I'll go back to my normal routine and pick up some long-neglected pieces of my life.

It was spring when I started writing, and now it is fall. I missed most of the summer, which is not a great loss considering how hot and uncomfortable it has been. But the people who paid the greatest price for my writing were the people around me who depend on me for certain things. Sara was often grounded while her chauffer sat at the computer. My dear Sunday school class often had to put up with half-baked lessons. There were more sandwiches served this summer and fewer family gatherings around the dining table (it was piled high with research). And no visit to my mother in Texas, who has patiently waited "until the book is done." My friends at the senior center survived well; I wasn't there to interrupt their card game, so their lives went on happily.

Writing this book has consumed my days and my nights for the better part of several months. It's not unlike birthing a child—a lot of pain, a lot of joy, and a few surprises. It's a curious thing, putting yourself on paper for all the world to see—the warts, the bruises, the happy dances, the goofs are all there. As I glance back through the pages, even I am surprised at what I read. I see growth I didn't realize was there. I see success where I didn't know it existed. And always I see the hand of God. I am humbled at how much of these words came from a Source beyond me. There were times the words tumbled out in sentences and thoughts that I truly did not even recognize.

Perhaps you noticed a few places where my tears stained the pages as I related stories that are still raw with emotion. I hope you shared my tears and challenges. On the other hand, you were probably able to catch just a whisper of the music of my laughter as I remembered the antics of three cute kids. I hope you shared our good times.

But beyond the stories and reflections and beyond the words, I hope you could see an honest expression of a life in constant struggle to find God's purpose through many choices and conflicts. In this long walk from my beginnings to this moment in print, I see that somewhere deep within my will is a determination that asserted itself in such a way that I endured. I have experienced the miracle of survival, and I hope you have too.

I would like to be remembered as a person who chose to live life, every day, to the fullest. I never want to waste a minute of this precious stuff life is made of. As I look backward and forward, I think of a wonderful phrase attributed to the great Dag Hammarskjold: "For all that has been, thanks. For all that will be, yes."

We are, all of us women, engaged in the same walk. We must reach out to nurture one another, to hope for one another love and laughter, smiles and sunshine, good times and happy days, through all the seasons of our lives.

Quotation References

Quotations came from many different sources; some collected through the years, some from new publications. Sources include:

The Columbia Book of Quotations by Women, Columbia University Press, 1996

Women's Study Bible, Thomas Nelson Publishers, 1995

Soul Searching—Meditations for Your Spiritual Journey, Thomas Nelson Publishers, 1995

Life with a Capital L, Thomas Nelson Publishers, 1996

A Woman's Book of Days, Thomas Nelson Publishers, 1996

A Place Called Home, Thomas Nelson Publishers, 1997

Coming of Age, Thomas Nelson Publishers, 1995

Forty Reason Why Life Is More Fun After the Big 4-0, Thomas Nelson Publishers, 1997

Mirror, Mirror on the Wall, Have I Got News for You, Thomas Nelson Publishers, 1997

"One Size Fits All," and Other Fables, Thomas Nelson Publishers, 1993

The Language of Letting Go, HarperCollins Publishers, 1990

Let Faith Change Your Life, Thomas Nelson Publishers, 1997

Only Angels Can Wing It, Thomas Nelson Publishers, 1995

Wit and Wisdom for Women, Thomas Nelson Publishers, 1996

To Mom with Love, Thomas Nelson Publishers, 1993

Potpourri—Uplifting Thoughts for Women, Thomas Nelson Publishers, 1994
Motherhood, Thomas Nelson Publishers, 1994
A Mother Is to Cherish, Thomas Nelson Publishers, 1994
Mother Teresa—No Greater Love, New World Library, 1996
A Simple Path, Ballantine Books, 1997
Gifts from the Sea, Pantheon Press, 1995
Too Blessed to Be Stressed—Words of Wisdom for Women on the Move, Thomas Nelson Publishers, 1997
Christmas Memories, Thomas Nelson Publishers, 1996
God Will Make a Way—Amazing Affirmations of God's Faithfulness in Everyday Life, Thomas Nelson Publishers, 1998
A Woman's Journey to the Heart of God, Thomas Nelson Publishers, 1997
The New Building Your Mate's Self-Esteem, Thomas Nelson Publishers, 1995

About the Author

Suzanne Dale Ezell is a freelance writer and editor, published in more than thirty different periodicals. A Texas woman born and bred, Ezell is a daughter, wife, mother of three, Senior Citizen director, friend, Sunday school teacher, and cancer survivor. She shares a special bond with all women who have loved, worried, overcome obstacles, juggled schedules, and with God's help are struggling to make the Walk meaningful.